D1394613

Darling, this book is for you, your daughter, your mother, your sister, your friend. This is for the woman you hear crying next door and the friend who is stronger than she believes. This is for the girl that you once were and the woman that you will become. This is for your future child and your long-since gone grandmother. This book should be passed from kind hand to kind hand, and its journey should never end.

"Wow... Wow... It should be every girl's go-to bible! Honestly, it made me cry, it made me laugh, and it filled me with hope, positivity and an incredible urge to live life to the full, to be grateful for what I have, to tackle what is not so good, to clear out my knicker drawer and so, so much more! You just about covered everything! I couldn't put it down."

"Your courage, your bravery is just awe-inspiring. Sally, you truly are the most amazing, beautiful, courageous woman both inside and out!"

"I want to give a copy of your book to all my girlfriends as gifts and I want to keep a copy by my bedside - it's a book I'd always want to refer to when I'm sad, lost or happy, to see me through!"

"You so eloquently write, with honesty, bravery, love, warmth and humour. I loved it. I love you for sharing with us girlies, your life, your family, all your wisdom and courage, positivity and worldliness."

"Every woman on earth should have the opportunity to read your book - truly inspiring."

Don't Go Faster Than Your Guardian Angel Can Fly

SALLY BEE

Sally Bee asserts her moral right to be identified as the author of this book.

All rights reserved. No part of this publication may be reproduced, stored in a retrieval system or transmitted in any form or by any means, electronic, mechanical, photocopying, recording or otherwise without the prior permission of the copyright owner.

A CIP catalogue record for this book is available from the British Library

Publisher: Media Delicious Ltd

Art Director & Cover Design: Tarik Halil

Editor: Tracy Lombard

ISBN: 978-1-3999-3591-3

Printed in UK By Adlard Printing Nottingham

Dedication

The book is for Lela who has had to cope with so much at a young age. Lela Loo you attack life with courage, sassiness and determination, even when the going gets tough. You are quite simply amazing and we all love you.

Also for Darcy, who we will love for all eternity.

Contents

1 **Love Affair with Life**

2 You Are Beautiful

3 Getting On

4 Breathe

5 The Big Picture

Introduction

The fragility of life takes my breath away. One step, one breath could so easily be our last. Yet we are all born to survive. Every instinct in our being is there to preserve us and keep us growing.

Often I feel like I am a character in a film. My character is being followed, pursued by a tiny infrared dot on my forehead. Whatever I do, wherever I go, the dot is always searching for me and I know that at some point, the trigger will pull and my curtains will come down.

Strangely, although I have been dodging this red dot for many years quite successfully, it surprisingly no longer scares me. Indeed, quite the opposite. It pushes me and pulls me. It challenges me, stretches me, it calms me and guides me. Because although I know I don't control the hand that points the red dot or the fingers that will eventually pull the trigger, I believe that I will always remain one step ahead, until the moment I choose to take a step back or stop moving. And until that point, I know that I am the only person who is in control of the weaving path that I journey along.

To know and to understand the power that I have over the wonderful adventure that is my life, is liberating. And so too, darling, is yours for you. Does that not take your breath away?

Setting The Record Straight

As soon as you are able, learn to drive and have your own car, your independence relies on it • Likewise, earn your own money and have your own bank account, even if you are married or have a partner, always keep some control, just in case • It's perfectly OK to make mistakes, as long as you learn from them • If someone tells a lie to protect you they are your friend • If someone tells a lie to hurt you, you don't need them in your life • Less is more where make-up is concerned • Candles are the kindest light • Don't try to please other people at a cost to yourself • If you have a secret, don't tell ANYONE, because then it's not a secret • Never be reliant on anyone else to get you home, always have an escape plan • EVERYONE has rolls on their tummy when they lean over • It's impossible to be miserable and grateful at the same time

The road to success is always under construction • Retail therapy works • Shoulders back when you walk, even if you are tall • Either go all grey or no grey, salt and pepper are for the table • Love bites and hickies are a no-no! • Never make apologies for being young and making mistakes • The world still needs fairy tales, so believe in them • Age doesn't matter unless you are a cheese • Be careful you don't slip if you have sex in the shower • It's fine to go to bed early so you can make the most out of tomorrow • Be different • Nothing goes right when you're tired • Be curious, always • When things haven't worked, it just means that you just haven't found the right way to do it yet

1

Love Affair
With Life

The Breakfast Club

As I entered the warm house, out of the frosty morning air, to my right there was an open brick fireplace with coloured fairy lights around it. In front of that stood a large wooden dining table with an eclectic mix of coloured glass candle sticks, mismatched plates and cups and saucers that all came with a history and story attached. The farm-style kitchen to my left was buzzing with female voices, laughter and a fizz of excited, child-like, energy. Oh, how I felt at home.

Eight or nine women were introduced to me in quick succession and I was handed a hot bowl of Shakshuka to take to the table. Someone had made muffins, someone else had brought rye bread. Catherine, the hostess made us all porridge (with rice instead of oats because she'd run out of oats) it was lovely, hot and filling, more like rice pudding. There were stewed apples and plums and we sat on a collection of different chairs and a wooden bench scattered with colourful cushions.

You know how when you are sat down at a table full of food, with people that you don't know very well, or don't know at all, there is often an awkward pause before people feel comfortable enough to help themselves to the food? No one wants to be the first to go - well that didn't happen! I remember feeling warm, loved and starving hungry all at once in amongst this lively new group of women. I started with the Shakshuka, dribbling it down my chin, I'm sure.

"Would you like a poached egg with that Sally? Who wants a poached egg – I'm making lots of poached eggs, how many want one?"

No one said 'no' to a poached egg, and none of us stopped eating to reply either, we all just put our hands up! Rarely have I been able to enjoy my food, in this primal way in front of a bunch of people that I'd never met. And yet we all did the same thing.

We tucked into this delicious feast with 'mmms' and 'aahs,' everyone cherishing the efforts that had been put into simply bringing us together and feeding us. And then the conversation fired up.

The energy for opportunity and friendship was palpable. Everyone had a story to tell, but more than the urge to speak, these women had a stronger need to listen, to understand and share in a feeling. This I find to be a rare occurrence, sadly. Most gatherings are led by the person who can speak the loudest and loves the sound of their own voice. So to be in the company of women who have enough respect and grace to allow each woman to say the words she wished to say, without being rushed, or interrupted, was at the very least refreshing and at its best, empowering. There was no struggle for 'air-time'. I felt both excited and relaxed.

Catherine, our host was wonderful at guiding us between the stories;

"Emma, tell everyone about the amazing project you are working on"

"Zelda, we want to hear about your plans to cycle around Iceland"

"Sally, please tell us your story and how we two connected"

Zelda was sitting next to me, actually, I would better describe Zelda as 'sparkling' next to me. Slight frame, bohemian style, with a loose-fitting blue linen dress, trainers, a tonne of chunky silver jewellery, dangly silver earrings, short spiky blond hair, the biggest smile you have ever seen and alive eyes.

When it was Zelda's turn to tell us her story, she spoke with a South African accent, a soft lilt with a big injection of determination.

"OK, Well. Let me tell you my story!"

She clapped her hands together, pre-warning us that this was going to be good!

It transpired that Zelda had been diagnosed with breast cancer ten years previously. Although her initial treatment was successful, the cancer had returned and was now classed as terminal. I sat back, in readiness to listen and offer sympathy.

No sympathy was required.

Zelda spoke enthusiastically about her life, her loves, her travels and how pissed off she was with the Covid Lockdown!

"This was supposed to be my dramatic time, and all of a sudden the whole world wanted in on the act and wanted the attention to be on them!

I decided that if this was going to be my last year alive, I wasn't going to spend it locked inside a house, along with everyone else locked in theirs. So I travelled quickly to Switzerland, I managed to get over the borders just before they closed and spent my first few weeks of 'lockdown' in a beautiful log cabin with the most amazing views of snow, mountains and forests all around. I kept running every day, moving and exercising my body to keep it as healthy as possible."

Zelda then made us all howl with laughter when she told us she was a 'failed lesbian'.

"I tried hard, I really did. After all my treatment left me hormone-less, I wasn't having a very happy time in the relationship I was having with a man, so I figured, hey, maybe I just need to try this with a woman instead"

She set about finding a lovely, gorgeous, strong and intelligent woman to have a relationship with. Frankie was wonderful and it worked for a while, but it wasn't made to last.

Zelda explained in the way that only Zelda can,

"You see, when you have a relationship with a man, have sex with a man, it is very physical. And then afterwards, you can chat for a while and rest. Lovely.

But oh my goodness, with a woman it's EXHAUSTING!

It's hard work physically, maybe harder work than with a guy, and then there are all the emotions to deal with. Two sets of emotions. Two people who want to talk on a deeper level, two lots of feelings to understand and support. Honestly, I just couldn't keep up. I had to go back to being with a man, I just didn't have the energy."

Zelda has to visit her consultant at the hospital every 3 months, each time expecting to be told that her very aggressive cancer has progressed, but each time she visits, they shake their heads in amazement, throw up their arms and say, they are dumbfounded at her resilience and they fully expect to see her again in 3 months.

I asked Zelda what her secret was. How did she stay so well? And stay alive? I was praying that she wasn't going to tell me she lived on alfalfa juice, and spirulina tea and only ever ate fully certified organic lettuce – and that was why she had survived past all expectations.

I can happily report that Zelda's 'secret' is held in her head. She thinks positively as much as possible, she LOVES with passion and energy, she drinks champagne and eats the best food she can. She enjoys treats of all kinds, however she balances them with physical fitness. She runs, swims, cycles and skis.

Zelda doesn't waste her energy on things that don't feed her soul. She gives her time and attention to the people that she loves, and lets everything else go. She holds no resentment in her heart, only happiness and respect for herself and others.

Zelda is not a woman who is dying from cancer, she is living the fullest, most rewarding life and everyday is a new adventure.

These women became my tribe and on that Saturday morning they fed me the oxygen I needed to feel alive. As I get older, I realise that certain gatherings are no accident, they are meant to be. The Breakfast Club now happens regularly and we are each other's tribe.

Finding Your Tribe

People come into your life for a season, a reason or a lifetime.

The beauty of good friendships is that you can be yourself. But remember this, there are different facets to being you. You have an adventurous side and a quiet, reflective side. You will sometimes find everything funny and at other times, you are filled with melancholy. Appreciate that your friends, just like you, are also complex and multi-faceted.

Wonderful friendships develop when you find the right tribe at the right time.

When I was an at-home mum with three little ones, I had a group of wonderful girlfriends who were in the same position as me. We spent day after day together with all the kids, chatting, cooking, playing, and planning. We became each other's lifelines at a time when our needs came way behind those of our little families.

Now, our children have all grown, and this group of friends has drifted apart a little. Not because we fell out or moved to another country but because our interests changed, our glue melted and we have all accepted that life moves on.

My children don't rely on me for their happiness and wellbeing anymore, so I now have time to spend on myself. This also means I can choose which tribes I need for different reasons.

My advice to you is this; make sure you are with the right tribe at the right time. Part of this is understanding which time on the clock face (page 88) you are currently travelling through. Be thoughtful about the people that help you feel energised and uplifted and recognise those who are holding you back.

The Breakfast Club is a group of women who inspire me and feed my soul. I don't know the family history of these women and that's not important. We get together because we all need and enjoy mental stimulation, listening to different life views and experiences. We don't talk about the mundane, we don't talk so much about our partners or our children, we talk about bigger picture stuff. I come out of these gatherings, with my mind alive, and my thirst for knowledge heightened. They encourage me to read different books and travel to new places. I love to be surrounded by people who live a different kind of life to me.

Sometimes.

But at other times, I need my lifelong friends.

I can count my life-long friends on one hand. These are the friends that I would call if something terrible or something wonderful happened. These are the first people I would call if someone had died or I had won the lottery. My lifelong friends and I aren't held together by situational glue, we are bound together in a precious friendship based on history and love. We have always been there for each other and know that that will never change.

These are the friends that know every part of my life, my family, my fears and my dreams. And I know their story too.

Treat everyone who passes through your life with respect and kindness, but take some time to work out why your friends are your friends.

If you feel uneasy or unfulfilled in some company, maybe it's time to find your new tribe.

Hang on tight to your lifelong friends and make sure they know how much you love them.

Be prepared to let some friendships slip gently into the background, particularly those that drain you of energy and take more than they give. Friendships should feel balanced.

You don't have to agree with everything a friend does, thinks or says, but try to understand their point of view.

DO tell your friend if her bum looks big in an outfit!

Understand that you can be your own best friend. You are often your own best company, so spend some time making friends with yourself.

My mum, Jill, with her tribe.

You're Not The One With The Problem

Words from Paula Rowe

"I suffer from Cerebral Palsy caused by an injury at birth. After struggling my whole life with physical activities and being bullied all through school, I found life particularly difficult. I also struggled with depression.

Life became easier when I realised that I had huge support from my great friends and family and that I wasn't the one with the problem! - the bullies were.

Now at the age of 53, I am achieving my dreams and doing things more independently. I finally have confidence in my own decisions and I see things through"

Other people's problems, that affect their behaviour towards you, are not your concern.

Remember that you can't control anyone else's behaviour, only your own.

You can't control anyone else's opinion of you, only your own.

So, if anyone tries to make your life difficult, always treat them with kindness, because you don't know what's going on in their life, but treat yourself with just a little bit more kindness than you give them. Because that's your job too.

Falling In Love

Falling in love is like falling asleep, it's slow and gradual and then BAM, it's all-encompassing.

But don't get confused. Sex is not always Love and Love is not always Sex. They are not mutually exclusive but, if you are lucky and patient, both can be possible together for everyone. But in the singular, they are quite wonderful too.

I find it fascinating how women and their sex have been regarded through time. Particularly by men.

If you haven't done so already, read Lady Chatterley's Lover by D.H. Lawrence. Published in 1928 but banned at that time in England and America on the grounds of obscenity, the book is unbelievably still banned in India today.

In the book, the fictional character, Lady Constance Chatterley, had to withstand a miserable marriage to an impotent man and subsequently had an affair with the gamekeeper and was sniggered at and ridiculed more for her choice of man and his class, rather than the acts of love that she and he enjoyed.

"Burning out the shames, the deepest, oldest shames, in the most secret places. It cost her an effort to let him have his way and his will of her. She had to be a passive, consenting thing, like a slave, a physical slave...She would have thought a woman would have died of shame. Instead of which, the shame died.

Shame, which is fear; the deep organic shame, the old, old physical fear which crouches in the bodily roots of us, and can only be chased away by the sensual fire, at last, it was roused up and routed by the phallic hunt of the man, and she came to the very heart of the jungle of herself. She felt, now, she had come to the real bedrock of her nature, and was essentially shameless. She was her sensual self, naked and unashamed. She felt a triumph, almost a vainglory. So! That was how it was! That was life!"

D.H. Lawrence preached sex as a kind of sacrament, an atonement, something that could save us all from the ravages of war. He wrote with a ferocious physical description yet also demonstrated an incredible wish for gentleness.

"Doing dirt on sex, it is a crime of our times, because what we need is tenderness towards the body, towards sex, we need tender-hearted fucking."

(Quotes from D.H Lawrence. Lady Chatterley's Lover)

Here's the thing: Great sex can change your life. Between consenting adults, shame should not figure.

Throughout your adult life and your liaisons, some of which may be slightly less glamorous than others, you will get to know yourself intimately. You will get to recognise the real you, your real sexuality, but be prepared because this might change over time. And that's OK. It's all OK. Whatever you are, whoever you chose, one person or 10, it's your choice and as long as you are happy with your choice in the moment, you have nothing to feel shameful of.

Great sex, orgasms, connection and self-love, are all some of the most com-plicated feelings we ever experience. Sexual actions have been routinely stigmatised, especially for women. Don't, whatever you do, allow your own thoughts to bring you shame. Have pride in your sexuality, however that looks for you.

And of course, love is love

Love is perfectly imperfect, hanging on and letting go, laughing and crying, sometimes at the same time.

Love is ambition and contentment, excitement and boredom, flabby tummies, dimply thighs, hairy armpits and ugly crying faces.

Love is glamorous, casual, painful, wonderful, horrible, fascinating, exhausting, time-wasting and critical to help us live and breathe.

THE Love Affair

All good love affairs have ebbs and flows. Love never runs smoothly. So accept that fact before you begin, and keep an open heart, an open mind and enjoy.

"Brilliant to look upon and to listen to, with the power to subjugate everyone." That was the description of Cleopatra, queen of Egypt. She could have had anything or anyone she wanted, but she fell passionately in love with the Roman General Mark Antony. As Shakespeare depicts it, their relationship was volatile.

"Fool! Don't you see now that I could have poisoned you a hundred times had I been able to live without you."

After they risked all in a war on Rome and lost, they chose to die together in 30 BC.

"I will be a bridegroom in my death, and run into it as to a lover's bed," said Antony. And Cleopatra followed, by clasping a poisonous asp to her breast.

As the romance between Anthony and Cleopatra played out in front of the cameras, it also blossomed in real life. The stars of 'Cleopatra', Elizabeth Taylor and Richard Burton shared a love story that encompassed two marriages, two divorces and a passion so intense it lived on long after they had gone.

Their tumultuous relationship was built on irresistible chemistry, vicious fights, a luxurious lifestyle and awe-inspiring gifts. They fascinated the public and the media alike. Through a decade-long first marriage, a divorce, a short-lived remarriage and a second divorce, the bond between them couldn't be broken.

However, it wasn't love at first sight. A decade before filming Cleopatra, they'd met at a party, where Richard Burton's reputation as a womaniser had Taylor deciding, "I'm not going become a notch on his belt."

In 1962, they came together again to make the film Cleopatra. Elizabeth was unimpressed when he asked, "Has anybody told you what a pretty girl you are?"

A connection began to build when a drunk Burton's shaking hands prompted Taylor to help him with a cup of coffee. Sparks flew between them when they filmed a scene that required her to gaze into his eyes, and an on-set kiss went on far longer than the director required.

Their relationship was volatile and intense. The couple both partied hard and drank heavily. They owned homes across the globe and travelled the world. They bought valuable artwork, a yacht, a private plane and luxury cars.

But considering all of this, I believe that Elizabeth Taylor and Richard Burton, if they were alive today, would say that nothing else mattered in the end, only the love that they felt for one another.

Elizabeth Taylor once said, "When I saw him on the set of Cleopatra, I fell in love and I have loved him ever since."

Whether it lasts a week or a lifetime, a true love affair, tumultuous or not, proves that you are alive, living and loving. Don't be afraid, go for it.

When love is real, it doesn't lie, cheat, pretend, hurt you or make you feel unwanted.

Sunshine And Coffee

In the midst of a love affair, when your heart is broken and tears have fallen, don't make any decisions or act on your emotions when it's dark.

Just sleep and wait until morning.

And in the morning, get showered, spray on your perfume, get dressed, put on your favourite lipstick and do your hair. Step outside and go to the nicest coffee shop you can. Sit outside if the weather allows, pop on your sunglasses, hold your head up high and own your piece of pavement. You don't need to explain to anyone why you are there, you don't have to pretend to be busy on your phone, and you don't have to make small talk or excuses.

Understand that you are wonderful. You are who you are and if that's not enough for a lover, then that's their problem and not yours.

Sunshine and coffee makes everything better.

Dream Big

You've probably been told that education is the most important thing in a child's life. I don't agree. Dreams are far more important than education. Of course, everyone has the right to learn. Everyone should be offered an education, but what is the use of that without a dream?

If a child wants to become a pilot, teachers should talk about the wonderful and exciting life of a pilot and the places a pilot can travel to. That dream should be fed and watered until it becomes a reality. It is that dream that will get the child to work hard at maths, English and science. A dream will spur a child on to get a great education. But if you never find out what a child is dreaming about you will never be able to hold their attention.

And that doesn't change throughout your life. My dreams are what wake me up in the mornings, they push me out of bed, even when I'm feeling low, depressed or lacking. And this, at the age of 54!

I think back to when I was 13-14 years old. At school, we were offered a careers session.

"So Sally, what is it you think you'd like to do?"

"I'm going to be an actress"

"OK...have you thought about becoming a childminder, you love kids don't you"

The careers teacher lived close to me and had seen me taking care of the neighbourhood kids. I didn't love them, I didn't hate them, but I didn't love them. I loved earning pocket money to spend on make-up.

"I'm going to be an actress"

"Your English grades aren't too bad, what about secretarial college?"

"I'm going to be an actress"

"Well, you do know that most actors and actresses never work and spend their lives penniless"

13-14-year-old Sally was the queen of eye-rolling.

"Sally, all I'm saying is you need something to fall back on, just in case you don't make it as an actress"

"I'm sorry Sir, but you just don't understand. I AM GOING TO BE AN ACTRESS!"

Dream Big

Having a dream is what will give you the wind under your wings and enable you to fly.

Your dream doesn't have to make sense to anyone else, as long as it makes sense to you, and you can dream big at any age!

You've got to dream about something so big that it dwarfs all your fears.

You can get rid of fears by focusing on your dreams, so much so that you will do whatever is necessary to fulfil your dreams, leaving no room for fear.

Your dreams might be sitting on the other side of fear and fear can freeze you. It stops you in your tracks and can paralyse you, so you have to go beyond that fear and simply focus on your dream.

I did become an actress. I worked throughout my twenties, appearing in small parts in TV dramas and commercials. Admittedly I wasn't Kate Winslet but I did OK. I travelled, I succeeded in earning a living and I achieved my dream.

Fear was always present in the background (mainly because at that time I listened too closely to what other people had to say instead of listening to my inner voice), but I chose to ignore the fear and do it anyway!

Thirty years later, I still hold the same dream and know that one day I will go back to this dream with high energy, determination and single-mindedness. I already know I won't listen to the opinion of others around me, as this is my dream, not theirs. And even if it happens when I'm eighty years old, I'M GOING TO BE AN ACTRESS.

What about you?

My Story

This story begins when I was 36 years old.

I was happily married to Dogan (pronounced Doh-an). We'd met when I was 21 and he was 26. We had 3 young children. At the time of this story, Tarik was 4, Kazim was 2 and I had a 9-month-old baby girl called Lela. Life was busier than it had ever been but I loved it, loved being a mum and the daily challenge of raising 3 kids under the age of 5.

I was with the children at a birthday party when everything changed. One moment, life was as it should be: we were happy, content and secure. But within a breath, my whole life turned upside down, never to be the same again.

At the birthday party, I suddenly felt extremely poorly. I handed the baby to a friend and ran to the toilet. I was overwhelmed by this feeling of impending doom, as if a big black cloud had surrounded me, suffocating me. Every breath became meaningful, as though the next one could be my last. I understood immediately that something very serious was happening to me and that it was beyond my control. I collapsed on the floor, feeling as if my chest was being crushed and I was struggling to breathe. I felt sick and hot and sweaty. The pain I was enduring was so much worse than giving birth to any of my three babies.

I managed to get back to my friends and what followed was chaos. An ambulance was called, and while we waited my kind friends tried in vain to help me – bringing me ice, water and a bag to breathe into. All I wanted at that moment though was to stare into my husband's eyes. I needed him to be with me and to understand what I was saying to him. I managed to give him some brief instructions on what to do with the children, but I guess I was telling him something much more than that too.

The ambulance arrived and the crew checked me over. They managed to calm me down a little and took an ECG (a measurement of the heartbeat). They said there was a slight abnormality, but because of my young age and the fact that I led a healthy lifestyle and there was no family history of heart problems, they were happy to rule out anything serious there and then. Even so, we decided that I should go to the hospital immediately to get properly checked out.

After a few hours of tests and observations, I was eventually allowed to go home with some indigestion medicine.

I spent the next couple of days recovering and feeling traumatised by the whole event. I couldn't put my finger on it, but I felt something had changed inside me.

A couple of days later, the pain hit me again. It felt like a herd of elephants stamping on my chest. Each breath was tight and so painful. If at that moment someone had offered to cut off my right arm so that the pain would go away, I would readily have handed over the knife.

My husband called for an ambulance again and events at the hospital started to unravel, like a really bad soap opera. It started with pure panic. I felt I was not being taken seriously and I was left alone in my cubicle, suffering in agony. I couldn't call anyone to come and help me because the pain literally took my breath away. I thought I might die alone in that cubicle and not be found for hours. Eventually, one student nurse looked at my ECG and her jaw dropped. Suddenly, I was no longer alone; the room was buzzing with people all around me. At one point I had three cardiologists looking at my heart trace chart. It was telling them that I was having a heart attack, even though they found that impossible to believe because of my age and healthy lifestyle.

The next morning, I was told by a cardiologist that blood tests showed I had suffered a very serious heart attack. I was relieved that I had survived but felt numb with disbelief. Throughout the day, I started to suffer more chest pains. I was monitored constantly as my heart rhythm continued to perform acrobatics. A nurse was sent to take a scan of my heart and I suppose it is down to my natural optimism that I still expected her to say, 'Oh everything's fine ... you've probably eaten something dodgy!' But her expression was grave. She has since told me that she was shocked – it was the most excessive cardiovascular damage she had ever seen in anyone so young.

I continued to deteriorate and was eventually wheeled into the Coronary Care High Dependency Unit. It had a very different feel about it to the ward: it was all white with very high ceilings and echoing voices. The beds in the unit had wide spaces between them to accommodate rescue teams of doctors and nurses. My team came to my rescue at about 5pm. I had sunk so low, the pain in my chest was breaking through the drugs they had given me and I could no longer talk. The only thought in my head was to keep breathing.

Breathe in, breathe out, breathe in, breathe out.

I convinced myself that if I could just keep breathing, I wouldn't die.

The doctors and nurses rushed to put needles and lines into both of my arms and each hand. They moved very quickly around me and spoke in hushed voices. I managed to whisper to one of the nurses as she crouched at my bedside and held my hand with great pity in her eyes. She said they were calling my husband to return; he'd gone home to be with the children for tea. I asked if I was going to die now and she swallowed hard before saying: 'Not now'. Then she gave her colleague a look. She was a lovely, gentle nurse and was no good at telling lies.

The team managed to stabilise me enough to move me to another hospital, where, they said, I would get fixed up. They had arranged for me to have an angiogram, expecting to find a blockage somewhere in my heart that was causing the problem.

I was passing in and out of consciousness. I was aware that I was just hanging on, and wasn't at all sure how much longer I would manage. We arrived at the new hospital and the surgeon, who had been dragged from his bed, told me all the risks associated with an angiogram. He explained the mortality rate.

The Cath Lab, where they were going to perform the procedure, was very cold and I had to lie on an even colder table to have the angiogram. By now, I was relatively relaxed, partly due to the drugs but also because of what was happening to my body. I was starting to shut down. I felt myself let go a couple of times and it frightened me, though it wasn't unpleasant. It would have been very easy just to drift off. I knew my situation was very bad, but the thing that surprised me was how calm I remained.

The surgeon started his procedure, putting a small incision in my groin. I felt the blood trickle over my leg. He fed the line into my heart to pump dye and x-ray the results. I was very close to the edge, but I was still quietly determined to keep breathing. When I heard the surgeon swear under his breath, I looked at his face and saw an expression of shock and disbelief, followed by panic. It was then that I fully understood just how dire my situation was, and in that moment I almost gave up.

I wasn't prepared for what happened next. The surgeon took off his gloves and left the room with his shoulders drooped. The nurses and assistants followed quietly as if embarrassed and I was all alone. I was alone on a dreadful cold table, in that soulless room and I thought for a moment that I was dead and that was what it was like.

I stopped forcing my breath and let my natural breath take over.

Each breath was so shallow and light and yet it was all I could hear in the room. I couldn't fill my lungs. Was I still alive? I could drift off easily and when I did the pain in my chest went away. I tried it a couple of times to see what it was like. It was fine. Just fine. I would then pull myself back and the hurting returned, but it had turned into a 'good' pain because it proved that I was still alive. I needed that confirmation. And I needed to feel the pain.

After what seemed like a couple of hours, but which was probably only a couple of minutes, Dogan, my husband, walked into the room. He was sobbing. He said that he loved me. The doctors had told him that I had suffered another massive heart attack; that my heart had sustained a shocking amount of damage, which could not be repaired; and that I was going to die. So as he walked into the lab, he was coming to say goodbye.

I would love to be able to write that I told him how much I loved him and we held each other tight but that didn't happen. Since I had just discovered that I was still alive, and I'd allowed myself to think for a second about my little ones at home, I was filled with an all-consuming need, desire and passion not to let myself die. I can't put into words how strong the feeling was. It was this surge of emotion that literally saved my life. It must have been all about the people that I love. It was instinctive and I decided there and then that I would never, ever give up breathing.

My recovery was long, slow and difficult. I had to deal with the physical fallout as well as the emotional. Physically, I was very sick for the next couple of years. I was weak and in heart failure, but my physical care was in the hands of my doctors whom I had decided I must trust. Recovering emotionally was far more challenging. I saw a therapist for a while, but I didn't find it helpful at that time. I can now identify that I was going through deep grief. I was grieving the loss of my health. It was only when I lost my mum, a few years later, that I fully understood the grieving process. Had I known at the time, I would have cut myself more slack to go through the process having faith that I would come out the other end. Hindsight is a wonderful thing.

For 12 years, I continued to improve. My energy finally returned.

Everything was trotting along nicely. My kids were all growing up, happy, healthy and thriving. Dogan had stepped back from some of his work as a cameraman, allowing me more time to concentrate on my media career, which was going well. During the years since my heart attacks, the emotional rollercoaster had calmed and life was on a more even keel. It had taken me years of 'working on myself to reach a point of calmness where I didn't let my fear of another heart attack rule my life.

I believed I had a future. Something that eluded me for the first few years after my heart attacks.

I'd had some tough news to deal with along the way. While looking into the cause of my heart attacks, and taking part in a research program, it was dis-covered that I had a condition called Fibromuscular Dysplasia (FMD). This is a rare condition of the blood vessels which caused them to be very tortuous or wiggly. It transpires I have wiggly arteries in my brain, neck, heart, kidneys and legs – the condition potentially leaves me prone to heart attacks, strokes and aneurysms. As there is nothing that can be done to treat this condition, in this instance, knowledge isn't power. Knowledge just means I worry more. I decided to put my FMD to the back of my wiggly mind and move along with life. I felt I had lived too many years fearfully already.

Then, in November 2016, disaster struck again.

I was walking along with Bob the dog and Dogan. I fell over.

It was one of those incidents that happened in slow motion. I face-planted the pavement and felt my nose squash into the concrete with ugly and painful consequences. Dogan tried to get me to stand up, but I couldn't move. The wind had been knocked out of me. I was aware that I was counting my teeth with my tongue trying to find out if they were all there. Then, I was blinded by blood. It was gushing out of my head and running into my eyes.

When I eventually did stand up, I went a little crazy, giddy almost, giggling and finding everything hilarious. That's what adrenaline does for you.

Dogan sprinted up the road to fetch the car and took me to the local hospital. It wasn't until I was lying on the bed, with the nurse stitching my forehead, that the adrenalin must have abated and all of a sudden I felt every bit of damage to my face and my arm.

My arm? A moment before, I'd been waving it around, now all of a sudden it was agony. An X-ray showed I'd broken my elbow. Over the next few days, my face turned every colour of blue, purple, green, and yellow. It wasn't pretty, but at least it wasn't life-threatening. Yet.

Six days later, still cradling my broken elbow, and feeling fragile with a smashed-up face, I sat up in bed and felt that unmistakable sweep of 'impending doom' wash over me again.

Having felt it before, I knew what was coming. The pain in my chest arrived. I stumbled downstairs and Dogan called the ambulance. We simultaneously recognised that this was a true emergency, neither of us said a word, and he could see in my eyes that it was happening again. And I saw that he understood.

The children were all around me, they didn't panic, or ask questions, they quickly got their school stuff together and left the house silently.

The Ambulance crew and a paramedic arrived and, again, I wasn't taken seriously. I had a laminated copy of my ECG on the fridge but the paramedic wasn't prepared to look at it. My husband called my cardiologist on the phone for him to explain my rare condition, but the paramedic wouldn't talk to him either. He wanted to take me to the small local hospital, but I knew I needed to go to a large hospital with full cardiology theatre services. After much pleading and crying, he eventually agreed to take me to the larger hospital.

Looking back I can't believe I had to fight so hard to get the treatment I knew I needed. I know I don't tick the normal boxes for what a 'traditional' heart patient might look like – but come on.

My treatment at the hospital was amazing. They knew all about my condition, Spontaneous Coronary Artery Dissection (SCAD), and treated me appropriately. I had a calm day and night while they monitored me and waited for the Troponin blood test results to confirm a heart attack.

By the following morning, I felt so much better and my natural optimism took over again. I convinced myself I had been too dramatic and that I hadn't suffered a heart attack. When the nurse came to take my food order for the evening I thanked her but declined and said I'd be going home before dinner. Or so I thought.

The cardiologist visited me soon after and broke the news: my blood tests showed I had suffered another big heart attack. I was so shocked that I felt myself contort, break inside and struggle to breathe.

I was suffering yet another attack. This was number 5!

At precisely the same time, Dogan called my mobile. I couldn't speak and the doctor answered the phone. He told him they were taking me to the theatre for an emergency angiogram. My darling Mr Bee understood I was in grave danger. I was bereft that he had to face those same fears again.

I survived the angiogram but the news wasn't good. This time the circumflex artery that goes around the back of my heart had dissected fully, causing a massive heart attack and more damage. Again, there was nothing they could do to help me, it was simply a case of wait and see and hope and pray.

I was devastated. I had fleeting moments of fearing the worst. Unbelievably, the notion that I might die wasn't my biggest fear. Far worse was the idea that I wouldn't be able to find the strength to battle back to recover.

I'd worked so hard to build up my strength both physically and emotionally and within a day, I felt that all my hard work and determination from the past 12 years had been erased.

I was back at square one. Worse, I was in minus figures because this was the second round of damage that my heart had sustained. This time, there would be no hiding my condition from the children. They were now 18, 15 and 13 and came to visit me that first night. They knew exactly how slim my chances of survival were. They understood that the beeping monitors in the hospital room were there for a reason, they knew the oxygen being pushed up my nose wasn't a toy and they understood that their Mum was very sick.

Dogan later told me that they had not wanted to come and see me, but he had explained to them why he thought it was important, as there was no knowing what could happen to me next.

I saw sadness and confusion on their faces. They tried to be brave, and so did I, even though I was so darned worn out. As soon as they left I fell into an exhausted sleep.

The next day, my cardiologists came to speak to me. They were preparing me for more bad news. They assumed that my heart would have suffered serious damage again and that it was likely I would be back in heart failure. Serious heart failure eventually causes death and can only be fixed with a heart transplant. I cried in my bed. I wouldn't let the nurses draw back my cubical curtains, I didn't want to see anyone, talk to anyone, think about anyone. I hated the world for doing this to me. I slept some more.

Day three dawned and I finally agreed to let the nurses open my curtains so I could see the rest of the ward. I wasn't happy but at least I was still alive.

There was a lovely old lady in the bed opposite me. She was about 125 years old, smiling, enjoying the nurse's company and handing out Ferrero Rocher chocolates to everyone that passed.

I love Ferrero Rocher and I realised I wanted one.

The gentleman in the bed next to me was gravely ill. He was slowly being drowned by his heart failure. He was struggling to get enough breath to speak to his daughter on the phone. He wasn't going to be going home to her - ever.

The cleaner came by; he was from Nigeria and had the biggest smile I had ever seen in my life. He sang to himself continuously and kept making himself laugh. I fell a bit in love with him.

The auxiliary nurse came around with the tea trolley; I had a hot chocolate and two Bourbon biscuits. They were perfect, totally delicious. I could taste them. I had a thought: 'dead people can't taste hot chocolate and bourbon biscuits'. I wasn't dead, I was still alive and I had this amazing team of wonderfully kind people taking great care of me.

I realised that I was the luckiest person on the planet.

I would have a chance to go home. I decided to get up and wander over to Mrs. 125 years and accept one of her yummy chocolates and have a little chat about the weather. My heart had suffered another trauma but it was still ticking, which at least gave me something to build on.

And build on it I would. I gave myself the biggest talking to ever! I dug so deep it hurt. I would find the strength and I would survive.

Why would I give up? Why would I think I wasn't capable? My family needed me, my friends needed me. I'm a very needed person! What was I thinking? How could I feel sorry for myself?

Come on now Sally Bee YOU CAN DO THIS!

As before, but this time more so, I understood that my recovery was down entirely to my state of mind in each moment.

The food that I ate mattered, and the way that I moved mattered, but the most important part of my survival was believing that I could. And I did. I still do.

The Most Powerful Words

Your life will go through a multitude of high and low moments. As I'm writing this book, I'm hoping that I've passed and survived my lowest moments, but of course, I know that's not true. I know there is more to come and I accept that.

All of our lives are lived on a tightrope or a trapeze, that swings from side to side and very regularly wobbles. Our job is simply to try and stay upright over the wobbles. Sometimes we just need to bend our knees a little to keep us steady, other times we need people standing on either side of us with strong arms, propping us up and preventing us from falling.

Your happiness comes in small, fleeting moments too and needs to be appreciated, quickly, before it passes and the wobbles arrive again.

When you look at your life as short passing moments, it's easier to understand the simplicity with which you should live.

You were born in a moment, and will die in a moment, and your life is all the moments that happen in between. Making each moment better than the last should be your mission.

Two tiny words are powerfully important to be aware of during your journey. Words that can flip your moments on their head. Everything, every word in life has an opposite, which always gives you choices.

So you always have the opportunity to choose either 'yes' or 'no'. Use them wisely Miss Bond!

You might think that 'no' is the hardest word to say, but 'no' doesn't have to be a bad or negative word. Saying 'no' to one thing can lead to a 'yes' to something even better.

Never be afraid to scream 'no' at the top of your voice if you are in danger. You have the right to feel safe and no one ever has the right to take that security away from you.

Shout 'no' in the moment, or carry it over, but don't let it lose its power. If you are mistreated at work, by a partner, on a date, or by anyone; keep saying 'no' until you are heard by the people that need to hear you.

When you are heard properly, your 'yes' will be more meaningful than your original 'no'.

A strong 'no' can set you free in a moment. A quiet 'yes' can lead you down a new path of discovery in another.

Saying 'no' to someone when they want you to do something for them, is actually saying 'yes' to yourself.

Saying 'no' isn't a question of never helping anyone else, but saying 'yes' with the right conditions is about balancing your needs with those of others.

Learning to say 'no' to yourself is crucial sometimes, especially when it comes to listening to your inner voice when it's using negative language.

Saying 'yes' to yourself is giving you permission to spread your wings and fly.

It might be a leap into the unknown, so you might need to just hold your breath and go for it, but hey, give it a go a see what kind of magic happens.

Your Gift

To be successful in your life you have to identify your gift. You have to pack it in a backpack with a pull cord, and jump with it strapped to your back!

Every successful woman that has ever lived, has, at some stage, decided to jump.

Life isn't just about existing; you have got to feel alive! If you feel that you are just surviving, coasting, existing but not living, not thriving, then something has got to change and that change will include a jump.

Everyone has a gift. It might be singing or dancing, it might be talking, teaching, writing, painting, baking, inspiring, supporting, nursing, or driving. It might be cutting grass, growing trees, cutting hair, it might be sewing clothes or fixing cars. Your gift will be linked to your passion and everyone has one. YOU have one. If all you do is paint furniture, but you are the best furniture painter in the land, then this is your gift.

As a side note – the reason some people can't find their gift is that they are busy wanting other people's gifts. No! This has to be your gift! Identify your own gift. Your own talent. Your own passion.

But you might not be using this gift to your life's advantage right now.

You might feel that you are standing on the edge of a great life, but you feel stuck and you can see other people flying around you, succeeding, living their lives to the fullest, but you, you can't get off the ground.

The only difference between you and those that have already jumped is that they have identified their gifts, loaded them up in their backpack and been bold enough to jump and know that their gift will support them. Their gift will help them soar.

BUT.

Understand that your parachute won't open straight away. Be ready because nobody ever said this was going to be easy. Don't expect it to be plain sailing. You are going to hit some turbulence, you're probably going to hit some rocks, which might hurt, but I promise you, your parachute WILL eventually open and you WILL fly as long as you believe in and use your gift.

Why can I make this promise to you? Because your parachute has always opened before, and I know that, because you are still here. You are reading this book – so I know you've got through everything life has thrown at you so far. There hasn't been one occasion when you haven't survived when your parachute hasn't opened. YOU ARE HERE. So, now it's time for you to be bold.

Of course, you can play it safe forever. You can continue your life just living, not risking any of the turbulence or hitting a few rocks, never stepping off the cliff but is that what you want?

Be bold. Identify your gift and do it passionately. Stuff it in your backpack and take the leap of faith to change your life forever. Your parachute WILL open and your real journey can begin.

Go. Identify your gift and get busy with it!

My Gift That Turned My Grief To Grace

Words from Jayne Clayton

"My brother John and I were like two peas in a pod. We were the youngest of seven children and he was the one that was always there for me. Waiting outside the labour ward when I had my first baby at just 17, there for me year in, year out through happy times and sad.

He died when he was just 52. I had suffered lots of losses before I lost John; my dad, my mum and my sister, were all gone. So I knew what was coming. But this time I understood that grief was a journey and that I had a choice about how I managed it.

The entire world was in the midst of the pandemic and we were all kept away from the ones that we loved. I wracked my brain to figure out what I could do to help myself and everyone else who was struggling,

So, I started to bake. This was my gift!

I set about baking some delicious treats and created little goodie gift bags. I went out every day, walking and leaving the parcels on the doorsteps of those who were self-isolating.

One lovely lady who had dementia didn't have the foggiest idea what the gift was all about but she happily sat and devoured the fresh cream scone in utter bliss.

Before I knew it, I had donated over 250 home-baked goodie bags and earned myself the name 'Lockdown Angel' from my local community.

I had found my gift and although the grief was still there, it didn't suffocate me. This time it felt much lighter and more graceful in its presentation."

I'm not an expert on grief, although I began to understand it as a process after I lost my mum when she was just 68.

What I do know is that grief is a journey that you can't control. You have to relinquish control somewhat and just go with it. Let it lead you for a while and certainly don't try to fight it.

I remember crying, a lot, after my mum's death and wanting the tears to continue forever. I made no apologies for my open grief because I loved her so much and I felt it kept me close to her somehow.

Grief is a deep sadness about a loss. You can feel grief for the loss of anything; a loved one, a pet, your past, your health, a relationship.

Grief, as an emotional process, has a beginning, and a middle and you usually do come out the other end. However, you may find that you are a different you - changed forever but hopefully able to recognise some of the happiness around you again.

There is a beautiful gift in all grief. It takes you to a place that you will never have been before and you will either be crushed by it, or you will grow stronger from it.

You may feel that grief will leave you broken, but remember, grief proves that you have loved.

I appreciate that any grief I have experienced doesn't come close to the grief suffered when a child is lost. In that instance, I can only imagine that my words will simply float over you and not even register and I would never attempt to give platitudes having never felt that pain myself.

Dotty And Connie

You are a wonderful, miracle mixture of traits and emotions, thoughts and feelings. Depression, anxiety, positivity and confidence all make up parts of your personality. None should be ignored, denied or feared. You need to accept them all, face them all and teach them to live side by side in harmony.

I know from personal experience the devastating negative effect that depression and anxiety can have on your life. It can rob you of your energy, your sleep, your memory, your concentration, vitality, joy, the ability to love, work and play and sometimes even the will to live.

There is no silver bullet solution for depression. Sometimes medication is needed to level out chemicals, and that is nothing to be ashamed of. I take antidepressant medication and probably will for the rest of my life, but I've learnt to understand that everything I do, think about and feel, I can change. I can be more positive.

This might sound hard to believe, but I live happily with a potentially fatal heart condition. There is absolutely nothing I can do about having this heart condition, it's part of me so I've had to accept it. I've had to change the way I live my life a bit, to ensure that my life is the best that it can be – but I have had to accept it.

Sometimes with depression, it's also a case of accepting it as part of your life, which actually takes away its control and puts you back in the driving seat.

You may never get rid of depression or anxiety completely, but you can improve your relationship with it, take control over it, and live a happier, healthier and calmer life, alongside it.

If you are struggling, I want you to accept that what has gone before, has gone. You can't change the past and we all can only do what we know how to do at any given time.

So, if you have anything on your mind from the past - write it down in a note-book and put a big, fat, red line through it!

Has anyone ever said to you,

"OK, you need to pull your socks up now and count your blessings!"

or

"Get exercising and that'll help"

Not helpful hey? That's because if it was as easy as that, you would be doing it!

So from this point forward, leave any guilt behind, because having anxiety or depression, or both, is not your fault!

Try to think of depression in this way;

I live in a small town in the UK, called Stratford-Upon-Avon, this is where William Shakespeare lived. So it's a tourist town, with theatres, restaurants and lots of visitors.

The flow of traffic through our small town is complex. Sometimes it gets completely jammed, other times it runs smoothly even during rush hour.

The roads don't change shape and the speed limits don't change, but the traffic running through the roads can be unpredictable. A simple thing like a flat tyre on a car can affect the whole town as everything grinds to a halt.

The north side of town can be affected even if the broken down car was on the south side. The people on the north side have no explanation for why they are stuck, they just are. Everything is connected, it's no-one's fault, it is what it is.

A similar thing happens in our brains which causes us to feel depressed or anxious. Something goes wrong, breaks down somewhere, and it has a very real, debilitating knock-on effect.

Depression is a downward spiral that gets stronger the further down you go. Depression is an illness. Anxiety is one of the physical symptoms. They often go hand in hand, not always but often.

So, here's some good news; with the right help, you are just as capable of being in a happy, upward spiral of positivity as you are of struggling with the downward spiral of depression and anxiety. You just need to know where to turn to for help. No one can do it alone.

It's OK not to be OK

Besides my medication, I have learned to accept and love both Connie and Dotty and this helps me cope with my depression.

Dotty is the name I have given to the depressed part of my brain. Dotty tries to overrule me regularly. She is wicked and whispers in my ear so that no one else can hear the mean things she says. She can talk me out of doing just about anything, she plants doubt in my mind about my abilities, tells me I'm useless, tries to make me sleep all day so that I enjoy nothing, she can force me to eat too much, or nothing at all, she doesn't care about my health, she only cares that she is in control.

But, I now understand that Dotty isn't the strongest part of my brain, I have another side that is confident, brave and happy. She is called Connie. Connie needs regular exercise, she needs to be stretched, woken up and challenged otherwise she becomes lazy and doesn't bother showing up.

Having confidence is one of the most empowering feelings you can have. Even if you get something wrong, if you are confident in your approach, it almost doesn't matter that it went wrong. However, Connie can be difficult to wake-up when you are being controlled by Dotty.

Confidence is a bit like your biceps. If you want to increase the size and strength of your biceps it's a good idea to go to the gym several times a week and perform a series of exercises designed to build up the muscle fibres.

At first, you might not see any significant results but if you trust the process and keep at it, eventually you will see your hard work pay off as the tone, strength and size of your muscles increase.

It's the same when you're trying to build your emotional strength or your confidence. Everyone has a Connie. You have a Connie. If she's been sleeping a while, give her a prod and a poke. Remind her of things that you have both achieved together in the past. Think about the tough times you have faced, and survived. Take some baby steps towards your dreams, wake Connie up and let her prove to you that she still works.

If you are reading this and there are negative thoughts popping up in your mind, and you are talking yourself out of waking up Connie, understand that this is just Dotty talking. Get Connie to shout louder! Dotty tells lies, you can't believe everything she says!

So, just like we have night and day, understand and appreciate that both Dotty and Connie have a place in your head. One is fun, the other is a sponge and will drain every ounce of fun out of you, but you can't get rid of her completely. You just need to take away her power and put Connie in charge.

One Day The Big Bag Will Shrink To A Purse

Words from Karen Williamson

"I'd never been a full of beans kind of girl. I'm much more reserved, always held back by a lack of confidence and feelings of self-consciousness.

Even after my much-loved son was born, I was only living a half-life. What was wrong with me? I managed a fake smile but I couldn't think about doing anything, I couldn't cook, clean, eat, or drink, I just felt sick. All the time. Everyone else was so happy. I just felt so tired and scared.

After 17 years of constantly struggling, I was eventually diagnosed with Chronic Fatigue Syndrome and depression. Being diagnosed didn't make me feel better, but at least I started to take the correct anti-depressant medication.

After one month of taking them, my grey cloud lifted and it was like a light had been switched on and the sun was permanently out. At last, I could laugh and smile and it wasn't pretended, it was real.

My anxiety and depression still get the better of me at times. It's like I'm permanently carrying around a black sack. I'm tired of carrying the black sack, some days it's a small bag, I hope one day it could be just a purse."

2

You Are Beautiful

Isobel

She walked into the restaurant as if she was walking onto a super yacht. Each step was taken with a quiet purpose and confidence. People stopped eating and turned to look.

Not classically beautiful but she had something about her that made her so.

She took her seat gracefully, crossed her legs and nodded to the waiter. He quickly walked over to her; his long black starched waiter's apron contrasted against his crisp white shirt. He approached her with the complicated menu in hand, but she declined with a slow smile and a raise of her hand. She didn't need to see the menu.

She ordered a small bottle of sparkling water, a glass of champagne and a simple omelette. She didn't want any bread but nodded at the offer of olives.

Her drinks and olives arrived quickly and she took a long sip of her champagne. She gave a happy shiver as the bubbles travelled down her throat and her head lightened a little.

As she waited for her omelette to arrive, she relaxed her arm over the back of her chair and took a slow look around the room. The restaurant was busy.

Businessmen in expensive-looking suits were enjoying working lunches, and a stylishly dressed couple in their sixties chatted about the last time they had been in town. Opposite her sat three young women, about the same age as her. They were excited, all talking at once, not listening to each other but just enjoying the atmosphere that girls together can create. Smiling, giggling, loving life.

One other woman was sitting on her own, about twenty years older than Isobel. She had out her diary on the table, her phone to her ear, supposedly listening to messages and a pen in her hand, poised, ready for instruction. Her meal had already arrived but she didn't seem to be taking the time to eat and enjoy it. She was keeping busy.

Isobel didn't need to look busy. She didn't want to pretend. She had taken her place at this table, in this restaurant confidently knowing that she was who she was supposed to be and where she was supposed to be. She had lovely friends, but she was happy with her own company. She had lots to say but didn't feel the need to fill in the quiet spaces. She kept her phone in her bag, as she didn't need a distraction, she wanted to savour the creaminess of her omelette and the bubbles in her champagne.

She put on her large round sunglasses, even though she was indoors and she enjoyed her space, her calm and her confidence.

Isobel

We don't know what Isobel's story is and actually, it doesn't matter, that's the whole point.

She might have been born with her air of confidence but it's unlikely. The chances are she has experienced struggles and trauma, quite possibly shattering ones, but whatever has happened to her, she has survived and it has given her an inner strength that will support her for the rest of her life.

If the scene in this short fictional story were real, and we were sitting in the same restaurant as Isobel, we could very easily misjudge her. We could feel a little jealous of her high levels of confidence, we might wish that we were as sure about our life as Isobel clearly is. But of course, we don't actually know Isobel's story. So it would be very wrong to measure ourselves using her ruler.

As the saying goes, you can never judge a book by its cover and that's especially true in this case. So the next time you sit and watch a beautiful, sophisticated and confident 'Isobel', don't judge yourself against her actions, as they may not be quite what they seem.

Vulnerable And Strong

You might feel that your weaknesses or vulnerabilities outweigh any strengths you have, but that's just not the truth.

You can be vulnerable *and* strong.

In fact, you only have strengths because you also have weaknesses. One cannot exist without the other.

Imagine if you were sitting with a friend, and they told you how well they are doing, how wonderful their life is, how successful they are at everything they have ever done; how would you feel?

Would you admire them?

Would you want to celebrate their brilliance?

Or would you silently be telling them to grow up, be truthful and stop kidding themselves?

Now imagine another friend sitting in front of you telling you about the tough time they had been through, the illness they had suffered or the deep sadness they had felt. This friend shares with you their mistakes, their fears, their vulnerabilities...how would you feel about this friend? Would you judge her as being weak?

Of course not!

You would regard this friend as being brave, strong and courageous. This friend has strength shining in her soul, simply because of her vulnerabilities.

The truth is, your weaknesses, your vulnerabilities and your past story are what make you strong today. Everyone has a story to tell and what matters most is that you don't fear it, be dishonest about it or try to hide it. You share it and indeed shout about it. Celebrate your successes, but even more importantly, celebrate your weaknesses, because they are what make you, you.

The strength that comes from vulnerability is as beautiful as you are.

Wendy

While I was busy enjoying my time working on a British TV show, I started suffering from hair loss due to some of my heart medications. Initially, I was devastated. I felt uber vulnerable.

I tried to cover the bald patches up for a while, using clever combing techniques (think Donald Trump with false lashes!) and lots of hair accessories, but it got so bad that eventually, I had to get fitted for a wig.

As with most challenges in my life, I allowed myself a little time to wallow in self-pity (we all need to do that sometimes) but then I decided to embrace Wendy (the wig) and enjoy the extra half an hour in bed in the mornings that Wendy allowed me because she was styled perfectly and took no time at all to get ready!

During the first few weeks of wearing Wendy on the show, I got so many compliments from people saying how fabulous my hair looked and where did I get it cut?

Hairloss is something that many women will suffer at some time in their life, so I couldn't keep quiet and have ladies look at me with a sigh of envy that wasn't deserved.

So, I took a deep breath and introduced the world to Wendy. I came out as a wig wearer on national TV, and in the national newspapers and spoke about her often.

I was fully prepared to be a wig wearer forever as I was told my hair would never grow back - But guess what? It has!

(Do believe in miracles darlings, they do happen!)

While Wendy was in my life, I went on a filming trip to Mauritius with 5 members of the audience of the TV show I was working on. My job was to help them lose weight and get healthy. I knew our filming days were going to be long, usually around 10 hours, so on the first evening, I sat with my filming mates and told them that although I was wearing a wig for filming, I would be taking it off during downtime. I felt a little self-conscious, so I decided to broach the subject and show them how I looked without it so that I could relax when needed. Of course, they were all accepting, friendly and non-judgemental.

I did, however, ask them not to take pictures of me when I wasn't wearing Wendy. I didn't think it was a pretty sight at all!

After one particularly long filming day, we all collapsed on the beach for a rest before dinner. It was hot and sticky, and we were thankful for the lovely gentle breeze floating over us.

I was lying on a hammock, one foot on the ground, swinging slowly back and forth.

We spent a few minutes chatting and then we all seemed to drift off into a restorative nap.

While happily napping away, in the most beautiful location, I clearly had a primal need for freedom!

During my sleep, I must have whipped Wendy off my hot little head and settled back into my comfortable position with one leg on the ground and the rest of my bikini-clad body sinking into the soft, rocking hammock.

I awoke to lovely, lighthearted giggles.

Wendy was now nestled quite happily and peacefully in my groin, making me look like a 1970's throwback porn star with hair poking out from every angle!

Miraculously, no one took a picture. Thank you!

I Think I'm Pretty Great

Words from Grace Haynes

"My Mum and I had a very strained relationship throughout my teens. Looking back on it now I never seemed able to please her. No matter what I did or said, I was always getting into trouble. No matter how hard I tried, I was constantly told I could do better.

I have carried this negative feeling about myself around with me through-out my adult life. I have always felt that I should be doing better, or at times I simply thought, well, I can never be good enough so why do I bother?

But I was lucky because I had another voice in my life growing up. My Grandma was my confidante and boosted my confidence when it was lacking. Although sadly my Grandma is no longer with us, she is always there in my mind with her gentle laugh and her wise words of comfort.

I've recently realised that although I can't change the past, I can reframe it, so that I make my lovely Grandma's encouraging voice, the strongest voice in my memory.

So, with her words still ringing in my mind, I am able to face my fears and my vulnerabilities and always seem to find a way through.

My past journey, both the good parts and bad parts, has made me who I am today and do you know what? As my Grandma used to tell me, I do now believe that I'm pretty great."

Clock Face

Life is one journey around the clock face.

We are all born at 12 o'clock midnight, and the first half of our life, between 12 o'clock and 6 o'clock is when we are led and influenced by everything and everyone else around us; our friends, family and teachers. We don't necessarily make decisions about what we want to do, we go with the flow and we are reactionary, especially when an opportunity presents itself.

If you are on the first half of your clock face, maybe you are 18 years old or heading towards 25, I have great news for you; you can genuinely claim immunity to responsibility for many of your actions. At this stage, you will believe you are in control. This happens without the burden or gift of experience. You are doing things for the first time. You are not so aware. Things just simply happen.

I remember being 17 and thinking that I knew better than anyone else. I can remember wondering how on earth my parents had survived this long knowing so little!

Our teenage years, 20's and early 30's are all spent in the experimental first half of the clock. We have our first relationships, and figure out our sexuality, our likes and dislikes, ambitions and dreams.

We all make loads of mistakes during the first half of our journey but that's good. We are not in control at this stage, life is in control of us. That's what gives us hindsight as we go into the second half.

The second half of our journey starts at around 6 o'clock. You'll know you are here when you wake up to the possibility that your life is a result of your decisions and actions and not merely what happens to crop up next.

You'll know you are at 6 o'clock when you can look back and recognise the mistakes you made in the past and accept them. If you are at this stage, you mustn't feel guilty for past mistakes, because there is no point. You are ready for the second part of your clock journey when you accept that you can control your life moving forwards. Your life is now in your hands, and although you still can't control what happens around you or to you, you have the power to control how you react to it.

I am 54 years old as I write this book and I consider myself to be sitting at around 7.40, so just past halfway on my journey around the clock face and this is where life gets really interesting. This is where I choose to take control.

It's worth mentioning here that I don't see the two halves of the clock as equal time distances. Just because it took me around 50 years to get to 6 o'clock, that doesn't mean it'll take me another 50 years to get to my checkout time at 12pm midnight...as we all know, during the second half of life, the hands tick quicker.

So, currently, my time is 7.40 and I'm loving being in the second half of my clock journey. Instead of just being reactionary and falling from one opportunity to another or rather, one disaster to another, I now choose which route I take. It's more than empowering.

When I was younger, if a job opportunity came to me, I would grab it with both hands, leaving behind a trail of unfulfilled paths, just because I believed it was surely *meant to be*. I didn't like planning, I preferred to go with the flow.

Now, at my 7.40, I make my choices before the opportunities are presented to me. I can pre-empt them because I manufacture them.

I feel ashamed to say this, but when I was younger, I often felt sorry for people aged 40 and over, you know, 'old people'. I felt sorry for them because I figured they must be bored stupid, not going out to parties and having exciting plans for the future. How sad that they wanted peace and quiet and sometimes to be alone. I was never going to become old like that! I would always want to party and plan and keep moving.

Umm, if I had the opportunity to visit my younger self, would I tell her what I know now? No way!

I see that same thought about 'old people' flash through my daughter's eyes now. At 18 she is enjoying the first half of her clock journey and thinks that anyone who has passed 6 o'clock is well and truly over the hill and clueless. I'm not going to say or do anything to alter her beliefs, because I know one day when she hits her 7 o'clock, she will understand. In the meantime, she can carry on blissfully unaware of what lies ahead. I hope she doesn't hit her 7 o'clock until she's at least 65 years old!

If you have not yet reached 6 o'clock, enjoy every tick of the hand, make it count and don't rush it. All the hours are wonderful, amazing and different.

Here at my 7.40, I feel excited because I've come to realise that I'm a bit of a magician and I can make things happen, I no longer need to go with the flow, I am the flow!

It's liberating to know that a good life is about happy moments, minutes, nano-seconds even.

When you are going through hell, reflecting on a past moment of happiness can help you take the next breath and survive a minute longer.

Clock Face

I wonder what I can expect when my clock reaches 7.50?

I used to think I was a really lucky person, I now understand that I make my own luck.

I am responsible for myself. And you, my darling, are responsible for you.

What time are you at?

What Mama Wrote

I'm writing this book from my heart, and part of my heart belongs to the relationship I had with my mum, Jill.

Jill was a force of nature, with a big attitude driven by her desire for fun and independence. She was happily married to my dad for 45 years before she died at the age of 68. She was totally dedicated to him, but also to herself. And it is this gift that she handed down to me, and I hope to hand it down to you too.

No-one else is coming to fix you.

You need to fix yourself.

Jill died far too young, it was tragic, but the legacy she left me gives me the strength to withstand anything that life throws at me.

Before she died Jill wrote a book about my life, as if speaking in my voice and these are some of her wonderful words...

"So, I'm Sally. I left school with a smile on my face and one and a half O' levels in my pocket. Saying that I left school might suggest that I actually attended. That could be slightly overstating the case. I did sort of go, but not sort of on a too regular basis. Of course, I had to put in an appearance occasionally if only to keep one eye on the talent, and the other eye on the competition.

To be honest, it could be a bit of an inconvenience, (having to go to school) but hot boys were a rarity, so any new possibilities needed to be claimed quickly.

Before an appearance could commence, a quick unscheduled trip home was required in order to ditch the unflattering blouse, tie and woolly jumper, hitch up my regulation school skirt to somewhere around my midriff and quickly dash back to school, leaving me out of breath from the unac-customed exercise involved. (Yes, I usually managed to bunk off PE too)...

I easily perfected the art of seeming to be in school more often than I actu-ally was, by being as disruptive and noisy as

possible when I did put in an appearance – thus encouraging the teachers to blot me from their conscious recognition, and having a cast iron alibi when I didn't.

Changing my hair colour on a regular basis also threw the teachers slightly off track; as did turfing out my friends from their regular desks, plonking myself down in their place, smiling innocently, and consequently reading someone else's homework.

...I left school at 16, and for a year or two, I had a high old time, and even had one or two proper jobs. Well, proper in the sense that they existed, rather than in the sense that I did them properly.

Now and again my dad would look at his bank statement and sigh very pointedly in my direction. He would tentatively suggest that a two-day week was intended for people approaching retirement, rather than for daughters who simply couldn't fit in five days of work around their social commitments. When this happened I would invariably go out and get three jobs, and spend the next few weeks demanding lifts to get me from one to the other. This, along with needing meals and bathwater at inconvenient times, caused my parents to heave a small sigh of relief when I slipped back into the old routine.

Failing the appearance of a millionaire boyfriend, I finally gave serious thought to the business of making a living and began to consider the options. I needed a job with reasonable hours, say from 11am to 3.30pm, with an hour and a half for lunch. If absolutely necessary I could stretch to 5 days a week but obviously not every week. Oh and it needed to be well-paid and preferably not involve anything manual which might chip my nail varnish. Scanning the papers and being laughed out of job centres eventually convinced me that this job might not exist unless I was considering a future in politics!"

(My mum had the most wonderful sense of humour!)

Wasted Time

My twenties were spent in a whirlwind of travel, photo shoots, filming assignments and personal emotional torture!

I worked as a photographic model with a 'curvy figure'. Classed as a 'plus size' model, I was a UK size 12, with broad shoulders and great boobs. This was the 1980's and 'normal' models were a diminutive UK size 6 or 8.

I definitely had insecurities about my body, which was often made worse by the business I worked in. I often compared myself to the 'skinny' models and felt inferior and bulky.

I was living in a flat in London with my then-boyfriend (now husband), Dogan. He was all dark brooding good looks, long black hair tied in a ponytail, earrings, and a passion for Tequila and salsa dancing! We were madly in love. All my dreams packed into one delicious man.

While earning a living modelling, I attended drama school in London as a part-time student and joined an acting agency to try my luck.

As I was still on the first half of my clock face journey, I harboured no particular fear for the future but I did struggle with a lack of self-confidence. I got terribly homesick when I was away, so looking back, I didn't make the most of all my travelling opportunities. Although I was working successfully as a model, my body insecurities were huge. I often hated the way I looked and let this rule my happiness in the moments when I should have been most proud. I questioned myself constantly. My acting career was going well, but I kept very quiet about it, afraid that someone would find out I was no good at it...that I was just acting! (Oh the irony of that one!)

Reaching my thirties brought 3 new dimensions to my life – Tarik, Kazim and Lela were born within 5 years of each other and my life took on a completely different guise.

I was an at-home mum, living in jeans, sneakers and my hair in a ponytail.

My mission every day was to get through the day with us all in one piece; my main job obviously was simply to keep the children alive! It was then a bonus if I gave them a fun-filled day that would send them to bed at night with happy little smiles on their gorgeous little faces. Exhausting but wonderful. I loved it!

My body confidence still wasn't great, but I had very little spare time to worry about it. I knew my body had changed carrying and birthing 3 babies in quick succession, (have you ever blown a balloon up and let it go down 3 times?) but there was very little spare time or energy to worry about myself which I guess was a good thing.

Oh, also, added to this part of my journey, were my first three heart attacks at the age of 36, which obviously threw a rather dramatic spanner in the works!

Then, to everyone's amazement, I arrived at forty. The doctors didn't think I'd survive 6 hours, 6 weeks or 6 months past my heart attacks, so to manage 4 years and be fit and well was a blessing and miracle.

It was during my early forties that I had some time to reflect on my life so far and I looked back at myself with fresh eyes.

Looking back through my forty-year-old lenses, it was clear that in my twenties I had a youthful roundness and a gorgeous glow to my face. My body was amazing! My boobs stood up proudly, my stomach was tight, my legs were long and strong, and I had energy, exuberance and passion for everything.

Why, oh why, did I waste any of that time on self-doubt? Why didn't I just accept that the job I was doing was well deserved? Why did I spend so much time wishing I were someone else? I looked back on that life and mourned that it had passed without my even noticing how wonderful that time was.

I had a similar reaction when I looked back on my thirties. Had anyone asked me at the time, the words that I would have used to describe myself were rushed, tired, casual, torn, worn and otherwise occupied.

Now, looking back from the vantage point of my forties, I could see that the words I should have proudly used were; energetic, caring, loving, maternal, surviving, strong and determined. Added to which, although I lived in jeans and a casual ponytail, I looked good. I really did look good. Another decade wasted on not appreciating the beauty that I should have seen in myself

So, in my forties, I made a pact with myself. I decided no more. No more self-doubting, no more self-judging. No more body-hating and decades wasted.

As I sit writing this book, I'm in my mid-fifties. I have lumps and bumps, wrinkles and stretch marks, but I'm also gorgeous! I can remember how I looked and what I got up to in my twenties. I also remember how much I loved bringing up my babies in my thirties. My forties were a period of reflection, recovery and re-invention and now I'm in my mid-fifties and I love everything about my life! Admittedly my body has the marks of a life lived, but that's OK, it is still supporting me and working hard for me, so I will love its imperfect beauty forever more.

I try to imagine what my sixties will be like and I hope that I'm still up to no good well into my seventies, eighties and nineties – but I will stick to the promise that I have made myself; to always love, respect and be grateful for my beautiful, gorgeous, imperfect perfection.

Whatever your age, don't waste any time on self-doubt. You are the original YOU and nobody can be a better and more gorgeous you than you!

Perfectly Imperfect

Besides her voice, Barbra Streisand is probably best known for her nose! And I know people often used to wonder why she never had it fixed.

This is what Barbra had to say about the topic over the years: "Well, first of all, I didn't have the money to have my nose fixed — even if I had thought about it, which I did think about it. The real reason is I didn't trust the doctors to make my nose right...I thought my nose went with my face, ya know, it's all rather odd."

Barbra talked about her nose when interviewed for PLAYBOY Magazine in 1977.

PLAYBOY: What is it, do you think, that makes your voice so special?

STREISAND: My deviated septum. If I ever had my nose fixed, it would ruin my career.

PLAYBOY: Did you ever consider having it fixed?

STREISAND: In my earlier periods, when I would have liked to look like Catherine Deneuve, I considered having my nose fixed. But I didn't trust anyone enough to fix it. If I could do it myself with a mirror, I would straighten my nose and take off that little piece of cartilage from the tip...See, I wouldn't do it conventionally.

When I was young, everyone would say, "You gonna have your nose done?" It was like a fad, all the Jewish girls having their noses done every week at Erasmus Hall High School, taking perfectly good noses and whittling them down to nothing. The first thing someone would have done would be to cut my bump off. But I love my bump, I wouldn't cut my bump off.

I think Silvana Mangano, the Italian actress, has the most beautiful nose there is. An incredible nose, Roman, bumpy, like from an old piece of sculpture. That's what I consider beautiful. I certainly don't like pug noses or little tiny noses.

... I do have a strange face. It changes so much from angle to angle. Sometimes I think I did look quite beautiful, and a lot of times I thought I looked really bad. It's a shame. But on the other hand, I'm not going to cry over it. I'm trying to be in the moment, and I'm enjoying my life."

If you are searching for perfection, you will never be content.

Who says what is perfect anyway?

The baby that is born with a gap in his lip; is that child not perfect to his parents?

The lopsided chest where a breast has been removed; is this woman no longer perfect to the husband she has shared her life with and who adores her unconditionally?

Perfection is nothing to aim for or to achieve because it doesn't exist and the sooner you give it up, the sooner you will fall in love with all your beautiful imperfections.

Perfectly Imperfect Part 2

As I've already said, I've always been a curvy girl.

In my 20's I was a model for an underwear company called Warners. They made underwear under their own label and also made items for Marks and Spencer. For them, I worked as a 'house model'. This is someone who spends time in the design studio being drawn upon! In those days I was a perfect bra size 34b and a size 12 in the knickers. So I would turn up to a session, ready to strip off and dance around in underwear! Not in a glamorous, Kylie Minogue kind of way, more in a test dummy, testing seat belts kind of way.

The designers would pass me a set of underwear to put on. Even this was a skill that I spent hours perfecting. Knickers were easy; I passed that exam straight away. Bras were a little more complicated. You had to do the usual, put it on backwards to do the clasp, then swizzle it around so the boulder holders were at the front, you would put the shoulder straps in place and lean over at a 45-degree angle and jiggle. The way you jiggled was crucially important. The idea was to let your breasts find their natural form inside the bra so that bra and boob worked together as one! Sometimes, I didn't jiggle in the correct direction and I'd end up a little left hand side down.

Next came a bit of manoeuvres and colouring in. Once I'd successfully jiggled symmetrically, the designer would take her felt tip pen and draw the outline of said bra and knickers directly onto my skin. I was then asked to dance, touch my toes, reach up high, and lean from side to side...in my head, I was doing this to The Bee Gee's Night Fever. I was a great little mover.

Once I'd satisfied everyone that I'd done every movement my body was capable of, I would get drawn on again. This time it was all about where the underwear had travelled!

How many millimetres do the knickers move on my buttocks, was one boob trying to escape more than the other, had the back strap risen at all?

It was fun, I enjoyed it although I somehow don't think that underwear companies go through the same rigours these days, as when I do it at home now, the staying power of the underwear is shocking!

I'd also walk in fashion shows for Warners, and this I loved! The fun and camaraderie of the girls backstage made me giggle constantly. It's a miracle we all made it out on stage in one piece. Getting ready with the make-up artists and hairdressers was my favourite part. It helped us all feel our most feminine and ready to step out on the stage. I have always been inspired by 1950s movie star styles, so I had a beautiful collection of dressing gowns to float around in backstage. If I had smoked I would definitely have held my cigarette in a long and elegant holder.

I continued to work as a photographic model for lots of different designers and fashion houses, and I was one of the first girls to be labelled an 'outsize' model. Yep, in the late '80s and early 90's a curvy size 12 was regarded as outsize in the modelling world. Unbelievable. However, I seemed to be able to work it to my advantage.

I remember one particular fashion show I was rehearsing for at the Savoy Hotel in London. All the normal-sized models were munching on their lettuce leaves and looking pretty miserable, while me and my outsize model buddies were tucking into pizza with joy and abandon. One of the *normal* girls came up and said she wished she could eat a slice, but if she did her agent would sack her.

I replied, "Oh honey, you should come over to our side, we get paid pound for pound so the more we eat, the more we get paid!"

She believed me. Ha - if only.

Now at the age of 54, with 3 children borne and 5 heart attacks survived, my view of my body is one of respect, love and admiration. It has carried me through so much and I'm thankful for every stretch mark, fold, dimple and scar.

Now I'm going to let you into a little secret:

Your body is, by far, the least interesting part about you. None of your friends loves you because of your body shape, they love you because of your spirit. Your body is there to carry you through your adventurous life, so don't let it dictate whether or not you have a passionate spirit. Do not do yourself that disservice.

I have finally learned to love my body. I think it's perfectly imperfect and I wouldn't change a thing.

My Endless Possibilities - Just Like A Tortoise

Words from Joanne Wood

"Communication is something I have always loved. Working in schools as a communicator for the deaf meant I was able to think quickly and interpret the spoken language into sign language.

I found this skill relatively simple until, overnight, my whole world was turned upside down, and I became one of those people that couldn't speak.

I was 45 years old when I was diagnosed with a massive brain tumour after I collapsed one day during my job at a school.

My emergency brain surgery was a life-or-death situation and I lost all my oral communication for a while. Thankfully my expressive communication was still intact, and I could sign to be understood.

However, even with my experience, my recovery felt very slow. I found it exhausting trying to process every thought, walking was extremely difficult and I found noise and lights frightening. I was overwhelmed.

My consultant asked me if I had heard of the story of the 'Hare and the Tortoise'?

The hare lived life fast, and the tortoise lived a slow life. The hare would brag to the tortoise that he would easily beat him in a race, obviously, he would get to the finish line easily because he was so much faster than him. Challenge accepted; the race was on. Indeed the hare was fast, very fast, to the point that he was so much ahead in the race, that he thought he'd have a little rest and snooze under a tree, with the finish line in sight.

The tortoise only had one speed; slow! He plodded along, taking in the sights, enjoying the journey and noticing his surroundings. After a while, he saw the finish line and the hare sleeping under the tree. He continued slowly, right past the dozing hare, over the finish line and won the race.

Life for me is different now, I used to live my life like the hare in the story; living fast, multi-tasking, and always ready for a challenge. Now I've happily accepted my life lived like a tortoise. I may be plodding along slowly, but my perspective and my expectations have changed. I now get to notice more, I take my time, and am more aware of each moment. There is still so much to enjoy along the way. I may be much slower and do the race differently, but I will get there in the end and believe that I can even win the race!

At 45, I can no longer work, or be in a fast-paced environment but I have learned so much. I realise that I don't need to be busy all the time, a simple slow life is enough.

I am not defined by limitations, but by my endless possibilities of life as a tortoise."

Your Signature Look

You are unique and therefore beautiful. You are the best person to be YOU.

I spend many hours watching women, who carry a certain style that I find beautiful. I like to gather ideas and inspiration, but I have learned to take those ideas and play around with them, changing them until they suit me.

I'm attracted to 1950's movie star glamour, Parisian style and classic, simple looks which were probably influenced by my mum. She grew up in this era and to me, she was the very image of a beautiful movie star.

I loved every part of her, I remember gazing at her hands and thinking just how beautiful and elegant they were.

Like my mum, I love everything French, particularly the independent nonchalant attitude of the Parisian women. I also adore Audrey Hepburn and although she was tiny and I'm not, I have learnt to adapt her style for my wardrobe.

No matter how your style develops or has developed, there are a few basic must-haves that I would recommend for your wardrobe. It's then a case of 'dressing' these base items to support your individual style. This isn't supposed to be a rigid list, you will know what you like, but I find that these basics, help me keep my wardrobe sustainable and affordable and still allow me to feed my individual style.

We all need a 'LBD' (little black dress) that can be worn understated during the day with ballet flats and hair pulled back. But come darkness, the neck can be opened, and jewellery and high heels can be added for a more sensual look and feel.

Black or navy cigarette pants work well dressed up or down, with high heels or flats. Make sure the ones you choose fit perfectly. No baggy bottoms and no 'too-tight' ankles. When you find your perfect fit, buy a couple of pairs to keep as spares. These will never go out of fashion.

You will have your favourite colours, but for long-lasting, sustainable fashion, think about going for classic colours that you can mix and match.

Black
Ballet flats, heels, bag, fine knitted jumper, trousers, dress and skirt

White
T-shirts, classic tailored shirt, summer dress

Red
Dress, cardigan/jumper

Plus **camel-coloured**, belted coat, **black** or **navy** blazer, **white** or **cream** blazer, **nude** low neck jumper, trainers/sneakers that look fresh and new not old, dirty and worn!

Accessories
Long scarves, different colours, but make sure they match your skin tone. Denim jeans, that fit like a glove. (Invest in a good pair, don't focus on fashionable shapes, simply focus on what suits your shape best). Add pops of colour with scarves, hats, gloves, and bags but never go too matchy-matchy!

Be brave and experimental and never be restricted by your age.

Step away from high street 'fashion' if it doesn't suit you.

Work with the body that you have, if you enhance your beautiful bits this will take eyes away from your not-so-beautiful bits (we ALL have them!)

Wear a mixture of new and old. Some pre-loved vintage items with a story behind them can be the most beautiful pieces you will ever own. I have a few that have been given to me and some that I've bought from charity shops and I love them all.

Invest in just a few high-end designer pieces that will last you a lifetime. Perhaps a small handbag, scarf or coat. Mix them with old denim, and classic good quality lambswool to keep the look casual but sophisticated.

"Buy less, choose well and make it last"

~ Vivienne Westwood

Iris Apfel - 99 year old Fashionista

Underwear

Your knicker drawer need never be overflowing! We all tend to wear the same few items over and over again. You know the ones I'm talking about, your comfy knickers, your lucky knickers, your period knickers and your sexy knickers.

If you have many, many pairs, I'm willing to bet my favourite bra that you never get to the bottom of your drawer!

Clear Out.

Throw away EVERYTHING that has a tinge of grey when it should be crisp white and throw out anything that has any underwire poking through. If it has a frayed edge or you have underwear that has never fitted you properly, throw them away NOW!

Have just 5 or 6 sets of matching underwear, (yes this is where matchy-matchy is allowed!) Lay them out in the drawer on beautifully scented paper.

Aim for

1 x smooth nude set

1 x black set

1 x crisp white set

2 x sets that you just love

Have an extra 4 or 5 pairs of plain black or white cotton panties/thongs for emergencies, but that's it.

As you are not buying in quantity, you will perhaps be able to afford to buy a few quality pieces. Let me just tell you that there are some really beautifully made, high street lingerie lines that are really inexpensive. Finally, and this is very important, understand that the correct-sized bra can change your life!

Feminine underwear is one of my favourite things. Develop a good relationship with your underwear because when chosen with love and worn properly, it will never let you down!

Each morning after you shower and moisturise, choosing your underwear is the perfect time to have a little chat with yourself about your expectations for the day.

How do you want to look and feel?

Together, classic and sophisticated?

Go for the smooth nude set, that is invisible under your outfit.

Classically capable with a hint of mischief?

How about the black set with little bows on the straps, underneath a white shirt and classic black trousers.

Outrageous Flirtatious?

Contrasting bright colours that are designed to be seen. Strapless bras are beautiful if you are showing a glistening shoulder. Comfort doesn't always have to be on the agenda!

The Essentials

Once used, never cheated on.

These are the products that I swear by and love to give as gifts to all the important young women in my life. If you are an aunty or grandmother, you might want to choose one of these to give to your niece or granddaughter as a special present. I have rarely been able to afford all of these items, So have on occasion, picked my favourite and popped them on my Christmas list so that someone else could treat me. Or, you could save up and reward yourself when you achieve a personal goal, making your *essential* even more precious.

Elizabeth Arden Eight-Hour Cream
Moisturises your lips, eyes, cheeks and anywhere that is a little sore. And yes it does last eight hours.

Nuxe Huile Prodigieuse
A dry luxurious dry body oil that you can buy with or without shimmer. Beautiful to add a sheen to your shoulders, arms, décolletage and legs.

Clarins Hand and Nail Balm
Smells beautiful and isn't greasy at all.

Chanel Universal Bronzer
Perfect for your no-make-up make-up look. Apply to your cheeks where they would be kissed by the sun, and dab a little down your neck and décolletage. Invest in a huge fat brush to apply.

Dior 'Nail Glow' nail polish
Keep it classic if you can...I personally hate false nails, they give me the ick. I'd rather see beautifully manicured natural nails. But who am I to judge? You do what feels right for you but always keep on top of the nail situation. No need for broken, bitten, chipped nails, EVER!

Save Your Skin
– Au Naturel

I have, over the years, just occasionally, been known to party hard.

However, I am proud to announce to the world, that I have NEVER, EVER gone to bed still wearing my make-up.

It's true! No matter how many cocktails have been drunk or how many tables have been danced upon, I have always managed to pull myself together enough to cleanse, tone and moisturise. Oh yes, baby!

I started modelling at the age of 15, and during my training, it was drummed into me that good skincare is paramount. Your skin is the canvas upon which everything else is painted, if your canvas is not in good repair then no amount of artistic painting can rescue it.

Having said that, looking *au naturel* for the camera is often far from natural, it's usually a result of dedication and hard labour. So, please, don't be fooled!

Instagram is a wonderful, time-wasting, dishonest machine. When you see someone looking *au naturel* in a picture, don't compare your own, very real-life skin with theirs. I've spent many hours in a make-up chair having plenty of make-up put on, to look like I've got no make-up on!

In 'real life', less is definitely more. Just a lick of make-up to cover blemishes, a coating of good mascara (I use Lancome Hypnose) and a slick of lip gloss for the finishing touch will usually suffice.

Botox, lip fillers, and surgery all have a place but remember that it's a privilege to grow old. Your face and body tell your story. It's great to enhance that but never deny it. The best facelift is a heartfelt smile.

This picture is taken wearing Estee Lauder Double Wear foundation, giving a lovely smooth finish. I'm also wearing false eye lashes, and I'm looking directly into the soft morning light, which 'bleaches' the skin tone and lightens the eyes.

3

Getting On

Raison D'Etre

Your raison d'etre, your purpose, your 'reason' for being here needs to be questioned. Often.

Why are you living the life you are?

Why are you with the person you are with?

Why are you doing the job that you do?

WHY?

You take your first blink when you open your eyes upon waking, you take a few deep breaths and then your mind gradually comes into focus.

How do you feel? Excited, full of anticipation for the day ahead or do you feel flat, dull, lifeless?

Having a passion and purpose in your life will bring you the excited anticipation that is so addictive.

Some nerves and self-doubt may accompany any excited anticipation, however, you can steady those nerves by taking a positivity shower (page 176) and re-arranging your mind.

When you own your passion and purpose, you will have more energy, and more fuel to power your mind and your movements. Your passion needs only to make sense to you, don't worry about anyone else. It can be anything at all that brings you to a halt in the mundane and puts a fire in your belly.

I wonder what you spent the most exciting day of your life doing?

Although I haven't got a clue what your most exciting day consisted of, I do know that on that particular day, whether you had slept well the night before or not, you would have jumped out of bed with high energy and a huge smile.

You would have felt young and looked younger.

The sun would have been shining even if it wasn't.

You would have felt strong, capable and in control.

That's because you *were* strong, capable and in control.

Having a purpose and a passion for that purpose motivates you to be the best you. It will change how you feel about yourself, drive your decisions and change your life.

When you lace together your passion and purpose with earning a living, magic happens.

Search for your passion and purpose as early on as possible. Identify your passion and then don't let your past determine your future.

Coco's Story

Fashion designer Coco Chanel is famous for her timeless designs, the Chanel Suit and the Little Black Dress. She worked with an emphasis on making clothes that were more comfortable for women. (This was in a time when all woman's clothes were corseted and terribly uncomfortable.)

Coco Chanel became a much-revered style icon known for her simple yet sophisticated outfits paired with great accessories, such as several strands of pearls and in the 1920's, she launched her first perfume, still iconic today, Chanel No 5.

However, Coco's early years were anything but glamorous. Born in a 'poor-house' and losing her mother at the age of 12, she was sent to live in an orphanage by her father, who worked as a travelling peddler.

Chanel was raised by nuns who taught her how to sew — a skill that would lead to her life's work. Her nickname came from her brief career as a singer where she performed in clubs in Vichy and Moulins where she was called 'Coco'.

Although Coco's life was fraught with trauma and drama, instability and poverty, she kept sight of her passion throughout.

Her purpose was to see her creations come to fruition and be worn by 'respectable ladies'. She made many mistakes along the way, which meant she had to fight to get back ownership of her, now famous, perfumes, but she always believed in herself, her purpose and her passion.

No matter what your background, you have the same right to your desired future as everyone else. Never forget that.

"Beauty begins the moment you decide to be yourself"

Coco Chanel

Never Mind The Doubters

Throughout my life, I've had a really strong sense of what is right and wrong - for me!

But as a young woman, I didn't have the confidence to follow through with my beliefs. I wrongly assumed that other people knew better than me...about me.

I guess I was around 40 years old when I suddenly had this flash thought; what if I am the person who knows me best? What if my instincts have been right all along?

Looking back at my life, I made some poor decisions based on other people's opinions. I don't beat myself up about it, because I only did what I knew how to do at the time, but the whole point of this book is to help you learn some of the lessons that I was a little slow in realising!

Very rarely do we know ourselves well enough at an early age to make the best decisions for ourselves. However, I recently met one incredible lady who clearly did.

Words By Margaret Whittaker, Founder of Slimming World.

"I founded Slimming World when I was 21 years old. At the time I had no money, no experience and no qualifications. I was intelligent but because I got pregnant at the age of 15, my education, which had been good up until that point, ended abruptly. I took small admin jobs on and off but had no career plans to speak of. Everyone thought my future looked pretty bleak. But I had other ideas. I knew that I needed to do something that I could control and that I knew a lot about.

I had struggled with my weight my whole life and I knew that there was nothing on offer to help people like me lose weight. I believed then, and I still believe now that people need to feel better about themselves before they can succeed at reaching their weight loss goals So I started a slimming club that would lift away any shame, guilt and embarrassment. Even in the very early days of planning Slimming World, I decided that we would never use words like 'don't', 'can't' , 'shouldn't' and 'wouldn't'

From those first days in 1969 when I started the company, to today, we help millions of members lose weight and we still don't use any negative language. I still tell everyone that they are worth far more than their weight"

Margaret had something really special up her sleeve that helped her become a huge success. She had self-belief. Can you imagine, being pregnant at 15, out of education and still determined to turn your vision into a global success? Margaret's self-belief was stronger than any self-doubt or the doubt that was passed on to her from others. Not only that, she realised that the language she used to herself and to others were of equal importance.

It's unusual to have that talent at such a young age, but it is possible. It's possible for you.

Remember that you are the expert at being YOU but watch the language that you use in your head. Being kind to yourself is the starting point.

Focus on what you *can do* rather than on what you *cannot*.

And above all, use your challenges, vulnerabilities and past mistakes as your superpower. The doubters are going to doubt. So, let them get on with it. And you get on with being confident, sassy, fire in your belly YOU.

Work It

Working to earn money is most rewarding when you can spend your time doing something that feeds your passion. It's not always possible, but I think if you can have a clear vision of the way you want to live your life next, then that's a great place to start.

I say *next* because we all need to keep moving along our tightrope. Whether you are planning college, university, first job or retirement, what you do next matters more than what you did yesterday.

Whether you are 18 or 81, having passion and ambition need never disappear. I believe that we need to find our passion even more as we get older. To do this as 'work' is when life becomes amazing.

Here I hand back over to the words written by my mum, Jill. She wrote about my escapades, including my work life, as if in my voice...

"Most of my work was photographic modelling but inevitably I had to have a go on the catwalk. This I thought would be easy. Sashay along within six paces of the end of the catwalk, smile, step left, step forward, smile, step right, two steps and turn. Sashay back again.

Unfortunately, the problem with this was that, not only did my mind wander (step, turn, umm, I wonder where I should go tonight, turn, step, smile, did I remember to wash my red dress?) also my eyesight was a bit dodgy. As a result of forgetting what I was doing and losing my bearings on the catwalk, I would occasionally fall off the end!

This didn't bother me as there was usually a hunky crewman on hand to throw me back. The clients however did sometimes feel that this wasn't the best way to show off their creations?..."

Modelling was fun, the best bit was the travelling, but I knew it wasn't a life-long career. My passion soon faded.

Next came acting, presenting on QVC the shopping channel, writing articles for newspapers and magazines, having babies, having 3 heart attacks, presenting heart-healthy items on TV, writing heart-healthy cookery books, training to be a counsellor, coaching heart patients, a little bit more writing (6 cookbooks published), ambassador for heart charities, a job helping people lose weight for ITV, cooking on the Lorraine Show, working for BBC, corporate health and wellbeing coaching, 2 more heart attacks, a few more heart-healthy presenting gigs, feeling like I wanted to stop talking about flipping heart attacks (I was boring myself) so started talking about menopause, more TV work, another book, daily coaching for women on Facebook, launched The Sally Bee Method, slowed down just like everyone else because of the pandemic....took a few slow, deep breaths...and here I am writing 'Don't Go Faster Than Your Guardian Angel Can Fly.

Every job I have done over the last 15 years has been part of my passion.

I've been afraid of so much because of my poor health, and finding my passion, my purpose, and using that for my work has given me a reason to get out of bed every morning, even when I've been convinced that it would be my last day.

Darling, try to follow your passion, always. And if you find yourself in a job that pays the bills but doesn't feed your passion, be proud of your survival skills but never stop dreaming about what the future can hold for you.

By Invitation Only

Your inner circle of friends will know all about you and still love you.

They will walk into the room for you when everyone else walks out.

They listen to you with the aim of understanding, not with the aim of replying.

They don't feel the need to walk in front of you, they are happy to walk beside you.

Your precious friends will agree that you are right, even when they know you are wrong.

They tell you, you were wrong, in private, when they are sure you can handle it!

They will lie to protect you, never to hurt you.

They will turn away from a love affair because he/she was yours first.

They will never mention the unmentionable.

They don't want anything from you, they just want you.

My inner circle can be counted on one hand.

Thank you. I love you.

Fearful Of Fear

There is nothing to fear except fear itself.

A few years ago, I reached a point in my life where I realised I was more afraid of living the rest of my life in fear than I was of dying.

I decided that I would rather die than continue with this half-life controlled by fear.

It was a year after my first heart attacks, and although I had survived, that was it. I was just surviving and existing, definitely not living and thriving.

I was afraid of everything, living like a robot. I was afraid to laugh, afraid to cry, to get angry or upset, afraid to shout and love. I was scared to move too quickly, I couldn't play with my children or with my friends. I was afraid to go out of my front door and at the same time afraid to stay at home alone. I couldn't seem to find a way out of the prison that was now my life.

Then came my tipping point.

I had just reached my first year anniversary and was due at one of my regular check-ups with my cardiologist. He told me that I needed to have an MRI scan to detect a possible problem in my aorta. This was a potential problem all along apparently, but as nobody imagined I would survive a year it seemed unnecessary to worry me further. But as I had reached this point, there was a strange air of urgency to deal with the potential problem.

They were going to organise the scan in three weeks' time and if they found the aneurism I would have two choices; either live with it, until it killed me or operate, without great chances of survival. Not the best choices in the world.

I felt like I'd been given another date that I might die.

During the three weeks leading up to my scan, I was incredibly agitated and felt I had to keep myself busy. When I wasn't crying, I was making arrangements, 'just in case'. I got all the children's clothes organised for the following season and I taught Dogan how to plait my daughter's hair, how to measure out the children's medicine and sign up at school for parents' evening appointments.

Dark days passed.

The day of my scan dawned and for the first time in three weeks, I was calm – just like the weather. The previous night I had been shocked by my thoughts. I realised that I had got myself into such a state that I was more afraid of living forever in fear than I was of dying.

All this time I had been looking back and not forward. I had been trying to come to terms with what had happened to me and was just surviving, not living. Now I was facing the day that my life might end and, it sounds crazy, but it was almost a relief. I suddenly realised that I just couldn't do this anymore. I couldn't continue to live with this constant fear. I didn't want to live if I was afraid of life. I wasn't being the mum I wanted to be to my children, I certainly wasn't the wife that my husband had chosen to spend the rest of his life with. Death didn't seem as scary as a life lived in fear at this point.

This realisation shocked me to my core.

I thought long and hard about my life or lack of it and then thought back to the Sally that had demanded her hair got washed while being cared for in a high dependency unit, and the Sally that made sure she had lipstick on even when she was on the critical list. I felt my blood run cold. OK, if today was the day my life ended, then so be it. Bring it on because I was ready. If I had to die today, then that was my fate and I'd be OK with that because at least the fear could end.

But. If there was any chance that I didn't have this horrible problem in my aorta, then look out world because I was going to get back up and kick its ass! Fear-less!

They told me I would be in the MRI machine for about 40 minutes. I knew I had been in there for over an hour because I'd been counting. And in my mind I was going through all the possible scenarios, the main one being that they had found the problem and were going to take me straight to the theatre to operate. During that hour I felt desperate, tearful, and sorry for myself, and then I got mad. I got really angry but somehow felt capable. I could do this. I COULD DO THIS! So, I stepped out ready to face the worst news, but...

...my aorta was fine. I was going to get to live another day. I could hardly believe the relief I felt. It was wonderful news but I also understood that this time, leaving the hospital, my life *had* to be different. I wasn't interested in living a half life anymore, I wanted the all singing, all dancing, loving, shouting, excitable, emotional rollercoaster that was not controlled and dampened by fear.

Finally, I felt free.

Often, your fear won't protect you, it can damage you and your fear is usually based on a story that you tell yourself, rather than the facts. The fact for me was that my aorta was fine, but the fear came from the stories and scenarios that my mind threw up and I chose to believe.

For you, a great life could be sitting just on the other side of fear, so you need to be bold, take a leap of faith and see past the story.

I still have fears, of course, my mind still takes me on scary journeys that are not based on fact. But remember what I've said about vulnerability being the reason for strength? Well, I remind myself of that often too. I change my focus and appreciate that everything I go through has the potential to make me stronger.

This, my darling, goes for you too.

Make sure your dreams are bigger than any fears you have.

'A Darting Fear'

A Poem by Emily Dickinson (1830-1886)

A darting fear, a pomp, a tear,

A waking on a morn

To find that what one waked for,

Inhales the different dawn.

Most people think they need more to succeed and be happy; more money, more power, more friends, more fame, more ideas, more stuff.

Have you ever considered that less is actually sufficient?

Imagine your life with less stuff, less stress, less debt and less discontent but more meaningful relationships, more time, more happiness and more space.

Imagine your life with less talking and more listening.

Less rushing, more breathing.

Less searching, more contentment.

Don't work hard to buy things that won't make you happy.

Don't exhaust yourself aiming for perfection when beautiful imperfection will do.

De-clutter your life both physically and emotionally to have less but live more.

Less resentment, more peace.

Let it go.

It's really easy to feel resentment for many things in your life, things that you may have, at the time, felt completely justified in feeling resentful about. Over time, that resentment might have taken on its own 'story.'

Whatever made you feel resentful at the time, is probably not at all relevant to you today. But you have been able to keep feeding the resentment, keep re-visiting it to keep it alive. Why?

Does it make you feel better?

Does it hurt the person who hurt you?

Does it un-do the wrong doing?

NOPE!

Choosing to let go of resentment is liberating and gives you freedom like no other.

When I was younger, I easily let myself be pulled along in life; I followed the crowd, let others lead me and always believed that other people knew better than me. Now, at the ripe wonderful age of 54, I happily realise that I am in the driving seat; I'm in control of where I place any anger and resentment. It's my choice.

Why do we hold onto resentment? Resentment and anger usually go hand in hand. If you feel you have been mistreated, you are likely to be holding an angry grudge against the person that mistreated you.

We all hold onto resentment because it's the only aspect we can control when someone has wronged us, betrayed our trust, or taken advantage of us.

Resentment is something we hold onto unintentionally, especially when we feel anger towards someone because of wrong doing.

Think about the reasons for your feelings of resentment; perhaps someone showed you a form of injustice and resentment was the easiest emotion to tap into to deal with it.

No matter how hard you try you can never change the past so there's no use in holding onto your resentment. By accepting what has already happened you can gradually let go of your anger and resentment.

Both resentment and anger are a state of mind and once you realise that, you can stop letting them control you. No matter how bad you feel, resentment is a temporary state that you can have control over.

No matter how a person has mistreated you, forgiveness will bring you peace instead of anger and resentment.

Forgiving others will bring you the closure you need to end the anger in your heart. And it isn't just forgiving others that's necessary, you need to forgive yourself too.

Forgive yourself for not knowing when to trust your gut instinct and for not knowing when to walk away from toxic people.

Stop blaming yourself for what went wrong and just forgive yourself.

If you want to avoid feeling resentment and anger at any time in the future, it's best to set boundaries. This draws the line on what you are, and are not, willing to compromise for others. This way you're taking proper care of yourself and you're letting others know how to respect you.

Your strength today comes from your past story. Nobody wants pain in their lives, but sometimes it's necessary to help us learn and grow. We're all stubborn by nature and it takes pain to help us realise certain things, no matter how painful those lessons may be.

While it's easy to dwell on resentment and everything that went wrong in your life, it's important to shift your focus to let go of your resentment.

Be a survivor, not a victim.

'I didn't suffer five heart attacks, I survived five heart attacks'

You've got to realise that you control your story, today. You probably couldn't control the 'event' that you were resentful about at the time it happened, but you can control the narrative now.

You can change how your story is told from this point forward.

When you can learn to let go of anger and resentment you'll feel happier in your heart. You will feel more at peace with everything in your life, and you'll be able to look forward to new adventures and wonderful new experiences.

'Go With The Flow'

A Poem By Atticus

the earth breaths deep and lets us go

the waves roll in and off they go

a girl smiles bright and off she goes

the waves roll in and off they go

love fills up and then no more

the waves roll in and off they go

sadness is here then here no more

the waves roll in and off they go

the sun comes out and then it snows

the waves roll in and off they go

the land is dead and then it grows

the waves roll in and off they go

we can't go on but here we go

the waves roll in and off they go

content at last and there that goes

the waves roll in and off they go

and so we battle trading blows

an old soul dies and new babe grows

time comes quick and then it slows

our life comes and then it goes

the waves roll in and off they go

Walking And Nature

Words from Hayley Atkins

"One crisp January morning in 2021, my family and I were out taking a beautiful walk around the countryside, soaking up the sounds and sights of nature. This particular day stands out in my mind as it was meant to be a day enjoying family time but this was actually the moment I felt my health begin to spiral down physically and mentally.

Over the next few months, I experienced terrible panic attacks at night, waking up unable to breathe and fearing the worse. Something was wrong with my back, it was getting more painful by the day and at the same time my elderly father's health was deteriorating,

That year, life was really very tough and culminated with having to endure serious spinal surgery, and my lovely dad passing away,

However, January 2022 saw me taking another crisp fresh walk in the countryside with my family. My steps were slower this time, my back was still a little sore but I appreciated every step, every cold breath and every natural sound around me. Walking and nature have been my saviour. We all deserve to feel good and to be happy."

Just like Hayley, I find walking in nature calming and often meditative. 'Meditation' is anything that distances you from your everyday thoughts. The action of putting one foot in front of the other and feeling the earth underneath you, give way a little, yet support you, is levelling and calming. When I focus on placing my heel to toe on the ground, and then the next, whilst taking deep breaths of fresh air, and listening to the natural sounds all around me, there is no room in my mind to think about worry, upset, anger or resentment.

But what if you can't access the countryside when you most need it?

These words are from Hannah Smith.

"I have a special way of thinking that gets me through the tough times when I'm feeling down. I think of my brain as a beautiful forest with vibrant green trees, colourful flowers, and animals moving gently around, eating the foliage. I'm aware that my negative thoughts are capable of dramatically burning the beautiful forest down to an empty, smoking, silent, black crisp.

So, when I'm struggling and having negative thoughts, I turn my attention to rebuilding the forest in my mind. I focus on positive and happy thoughts and watch them feed and water the forest. I can see the colour return from the ground up. I watch the flowers grow again, the animals come back slowly and tentatively, but then settle into safety and happiness and the sounds of the forest return like a quiet musical that never ends."

24

Breathe

Fill Up

Now, although this isn't a recipe book, I cannot write for you without mentioning food.

Every mouthful you eat has the ability to either harm you or heal you. Of course, you will and should enjoy plenty of treats, but you must also be mindful of taking care of your health.

My past healthy eating habits became my insurance policy when things went wrong. I helped myself survive 5 heart attacks by treating my body with respect and love over the years, and you must do that too. If you are young, you won't be thinking about poor health in the future, but I would like you to understand that it's a privilege to grow old. One day it will happen to you, so look after your body now like the precious jewel it is.

If you are older reading this, know that it's never too late to change. If you want to feel good and look good, the food you eat is powerful medicine.

My family and I, have often had to live on a tight budget, and if you do too, you don't have to let this stop you from eating a healthy diet. Buy your ingredients when they are on special offer and shop at the end of the day, when fresh items are often reduced. You can bulk up meals by using pasta, lentils and pulses, all of which are inexpensive to buy.

Don't beat yourself up trying to buy 'organic' or perfect-looking products; a vegetable is a vegetable no matter what kind of wonky shape it is - just wash it well!

The items that I am listing for you, should be your non-negotiables, so that you can take the best care of your health. When you have good health anything is possible, but when your health is threatened life becomes much more challenging.

No chemicals are needed in your food so cut out the processed rubbish (very expensive too) and simply eat fresh as often as possible.

Think about the food you would feed a young child, and treat yourself with the same respect.

Don't kid yourself you are being healthy when you're not. Ditch the 'diet' drinks because they contain harmful chemicals and when you are thirsty drink water!

When you have a treat, make it worthwhile. Eat a delicious Canelé with its thick caramelised crust from a French Patisserie, not a dried-up old muffin from the supermarket.

Don't get caught out. Planning ahead is key. Pre-empt your hunger because it will always pop up and that's when you are likely to grab an unhealthy snack.

Read the ingredients on the back, not the marketing on the front.

Spend the longest time in the fresh produce aisles at the supermarket. Buy a rainbow of fruit & vegetables. Try to hit every colour.

Try to buy local produce when it's in season.

Stock your freezer with frozen fruit & vegetables. They are often fresher than 'fresh' as they are picked and frozen super quickly and are perfect to cut down on expense and waste especially if you are cooking for one.

Buy:

Frozen chopped onions
Frozen peppers
Frozen garlic, ginger and herbs
Frozen mixed red berries to make smoothies.

If you eat meat and seafood, eat them in their most natural state. Buy from a fishmonger or reputable butcher who can tell you where their meat comes from. Buy in-expensive cuts of meat and cut off any visible fat. Buy Salmon steaks when they are on offer and pop them in the freezer.

Quality dairy products can provide much-needed calcium as well as protein. They are something that should be included on your healthy food list. Many dairy foods contain high amounts of saturated fats, so that is something to be aware of.

Low-fat milk
Eggs
Low-fat plain yogurt
Low-fat Greek yogurt
Low-fat crème fraish
Low-fat cottage cheese
Feta cheese
Mature cheddar
Mozzarella balls

Avoid cheeses that are processed and shredded or made to look like string! Yoghurt is another popular dairy food that can be a nutritional pitfall due to its added sugar content. So try to avoid yoghurts that are ready sweetened and add your own fruit and honey to plain low-fat yoghurts.

When shopping for bread, look for the ones labelled:

100% Wholegrain
100% Stone ground wholewheat
Stone ground wholegrain

If you have problems digesting bread, it might be the type of bread you are eating. Mass-produced loaves aren't, in my opinion, given time to prove properly, so much of the fermenting happens in your stomach!

Try bread that is made using French flour and yeast and is allowed to prove without being rushed.

Eat beans and lentils more than you eat meat! They are super affordable, filling and a great source of fibre:

Black beans
Chickpeas
Green peas
Kidney beans
Lentils
Pinto beans
Butter beans
Cannellini beans
Soy (edamame) beans (fresh or frozen)

If you buy ready-cooked tinned beans or pulses, rinse well before using.

When buying oils, look for ones that are labelled 'Extra virgin', 'Cold pressed', or 'Unrefined'.

The less processed the oil is, the better it will be for you:

Extra virgin olive oil
Flaxseed oil
Rapeseed oil
Peanut oil
Sesame oil

Nuts & seeds are brilliant to have on hand to pre-empt hunger. Especially when travelling.

Raw or roasted nuts are all quality additions to your healthy food list:

Almonds
Brazil nuts
Hazelnuts
Macadamia nuts
Peanuts
Pecans
Pistachios
Pumpkin seeds
Sunflower seeds

In addition to enhancing flavours, some natural condiments can also speed up the body's metabolism as well as improve the digestion process. So, feel free to add any of these items to your list:

Horseradish
Low-fat hummus
Mustard (French, English, Dijon, wholegrain)
Low-salt soy sauce
Vinegar (apple cider, balsamic, red wine, rice wine)
Honey

It's always nice to use fresh herbs and spices when you are cooking, but have dried on hand as well:

Black pepper
Tabasco
Italian seasoning
Cajun seasoning
Smoked paprika
Celery salt
Garlic fresh/granules/powder/paste
Dried bay leaves
Curry powder
Turmeric
Chinese five spice
Mild chilli powder
Chilli flakes
Garam masala
Oregano
Basil
Thyme
Tarragon
Cinnamon
Ginger
Mixed spice

Extras to have in your cupboard/fridge:

Tinned chopped tomatoes
Tuna fish in spring water
Egg noodles
Rice noodles
Whole-wheat pasta
Tomato puree
Tomato pasatta
Pesto
Ready-rolled puff pastry

A healthy food shopping list is essential to creating a healthy meal plan. It is also a good tool for stocking your pantry and cabinets with quality wholesome foods. Most importantly, it is a good tool to keep your costs down and to stay focused on purchasing the items you actually need once you are at the supermarket.

Less is more.

You don't need a pantry and fridge overflowing with food, especially when you eat freshly and simply. Just have what you need on hand, and replace it when it's gone.

Eating a healthy diet is one of the most positive actions you can take to help you live a good life.

The healthier you can eat from a young age, the more money you will have in your 'health bank'

Your thoughts really matter too...

Positivity Part 1

If you want your life to be better you need to be more positive. Yep, the answer to a better life is as simple as that.

Any philosopher will tell you, and I am always harping on about this, that you cannot control what happens around you, the only thing you can control is how you react to it.

There we go, life sorted. Ha! If only it was as easy as that.

When you are struggling with life, it's really difficult to become that positive person that you hope is hiding somewhere deep down inside.

You'll see people who seem to simply and easily breeze through life, always happy and smiling and getting what they want. They are that positive person you want to be.

But, it's easy to be positive when you are positive.

Does that make sense?

Just like it's easy to make money when you have some money because then you can invest a little and take a few risks to make some more. But if your pot is almost empty, you can't take any risks to fill it up, because you literally need every penny to survive.

And actually, that's the same with positivity too. If you want to be the positive person of which you've seen glimpses, you need to invest and take a few chances which can be scary when you don't have deep reserves. And you probably feel like you want to protect any shreds of positivity you have because that's all you have.

But you have to trust me when I tell you that holding back your positivity out of fear is not the right approach.

If you want an abundance of positivity in your life, you need to feed it, daily. Just like your body with healthy food.

Nurture your positivity, love and grow it, so that it can become the strongest part of your personality.

How do I know that having positivity will change your life? Because positivity saved mine and continues to be the driving force behind every breath I take today.

Not only did having a positive mindset literally save my life, it now helps make every day that I live, a little bit better.

You have a choice. You can't change where you were born or who you were born to. You can't change what upbringing you had or the chemistry or genes that have given you cancer or heart disease.

But you can choose what kind of life you live. You can choose how you react to everything that happens in your life and around it.

In times of crisis, if you can find the positives, they will be the gifts that change your life.

Welcome to my world.

Positivity Part 2 (The Positivity Shower)

My natural 'default' setting each morning when I wake up is one tinged with depression and worry, usually about my health.

'Is today the day, when it all goes wrong again?'

I could let that mindset rule my life, but every day I choose not to.

Of course, I can't change my health history, nor can I change the depressive (Dotty) part of my brain that shares space in my head; but my approach, my feelings and my positivity certainly can change.

I take at least 10 minutes of 'me' time in the shower each morning.

I let the water wash over me and imagine it to be filled with positivity and happy thoughts, it washes away my fears and my negative thoughts.

I change the way I think in a very deliberate way.

I picture my fearful thoughts being washed down the plug hole to be replaced by thoughts that make me smile, happy, feel light, trouble-free and positive.

As a human being, you are very clever - but not so clever that you can feel two emotions at once. If you are wondering what you are feeling, focus on what you're thinking. They are the same thing. So, to change how you feel, literally wash away the thoughts that are bringing you down and replace them with positive thoughts. This in turn will help boost your positivity tank and once you've got the first drips of positivity taking hold, it's easier to invest in more!

Stress Doesn't Go With Your Outfit

Whenever I used to hear people talk about meditation, I conjured up an image in my head of people wearing long, cotton 'hippy pants' with unshaven legs and armpits, sitting in the lotus position, 'ohmming' and 'ahhing'.

Clearly, I didn't get it at all.

My first experience of meditation was at the age of 36, after my first set of heart attacks. I was afraid to be in the house on my own, in case anything happened to me. The children were all very small, and I was genuinely afraid that I would die, and the kids would be left in the house, without being able to call for help. This was a very real prospect and fear for me.

So, for the first 6 months or so, I made sure I was never on my own. One evening, however, Dogan had to pop across the road to the shop to pick up some milk. He said he'd be just 5 minutes.

The moment I heard the door close behind him, something really strange happened to me, physically.

All of a sudden, I was aware of my irregular heartbeat. My chest started to hurt, my breathing became quick and laboured and I got pins and needles in my fingers.

I went into a complete meltdown.

This was it, I thought.

It was happening again.

I was having another heart attack. Typical that this had to happen just when Dogan had left the house!

I sat down, holding my chest, panic was written all over my face, thinking through the conversation that I was about to have with the 999 operators. Just at that moment, Dogan came back into the house.

I begin to cry and tell him I was having another heart attack. But as I got all my words out, along with my fearful tears, the very real pains that I had been suffering, subsided. My breath became steadier and my heart returned to a more normal rhythm.

The way that our minds and bodies work together is amazing. I had actually suffered the first, of many, panic attacks. The pain I felt was real. My heart rate did speed up and I wasn't getting enough blood and oxygen around my body which explained the pins and needles in my fingers. But this attack hadn't ignited in my heart, it had ignited in my head.

My physical reactions were real, but they started as a mere thought.

The next day I spoke with a counsellor friend. I told her what had happened. She wasn't at all surprised.

"Sally, the next time your mind tries to take you on a journey of panic, just feel the earth under your feet, touch skin on skin and breathe"

She was instructing me to meditate. And I didn't have to grow the hair under my armpits for it to work!

How to do it.

Meditation is simply a process to help you step back from your situation and look at it from a different perspective.

Imagine you are driving along in a car, and the traffic comes to a standstill. Thirty minutes later, you're still in the same position having made no progress on your journey.

You feel yourself get agitated and angry. Your heart rate speeds up, your blood pressure rises, and your fists clench. You want to scream!

But then you close your eyes and take a couple of deep slow breaths, counting to four as you breathe in, holding that breath for the count of four, letting it out slowly for four and then pausing your breath for another count of four.

Your heart rate slows.

You take another big breath in for the count of four to fill the very corners of your lungs. You hold it for the count of four and let it go slowly, feeling the air pass your lips.

You tap your two index fingers together and bring your focus to the feeling of skin touching skin. This is you. You are complete.

Now you imagine that you are floating upwards outside of your body, hovering a few feet above your car. Lightweight in a warm breeze. Close up and in the far distance, you can see other cars at a standstill. You see people walking on the pavement, you watch six birds fly above you in an arrow formation. You breathe in again for the count of four. As you hold your breath, you can see just beyond your line of traffic. There is a breakdown vehicle getting ready to tow away a broken down car; Ah, the reason for your hold up. As you slowly let out your breath again, you gently float back down into yourself, sitting in your car.

You are relaxed.

Your heart rate is slow, your blood pressure is healthy and you trust that the traffic will get moving again soon.

This is meditation.

Gaining a new perspective from a calm place can take you away from stress.

Use meditation to help you sleep, and help you cope with anxiety, panic and pain.

Just feel your feet on the earth to feel grounded. Touch your skin onto your skin to know that you are complete and breathe deeply and slowly. Bring all of your attention to each breath as it enters and leaves your body.

You are doing great.

Strike A Pose

If you have practised some meditation and found that floating overhead to distance yourself from your stress works for you, you might want to take it to another level.

I have recently discovered Tai Chi. A free-flowing movement form of meditation that certainly helps me feel calm yet energised. It relaxes me but also enhances the flow of energy through my body.

It's actually amazing!

The deep breathing practised in Tai Chi uses the full extent of your lung capacity, and the gentle stretching poses, bring much-needed flexibility and tone.

Give it a go, either in a group, or in the privacy of your back garden. I really recommend you do.

The following words are from Suzy Elrick.

"I call it my awakening.

After an enormous life scare at the age of 21, I began to prepare for a more healthy future life. I have always felt I had a strong understanding of myself. Reflection was part of my life, I knew what was important, I felt contentment and had a desire to guide other people to recognise this strength in themselves. But I struggled to feel the freedom that I desired.

When I found a type of Tai Chi called Taoist, I finally felt connected with other kindred spirits. I didn't want to leave the first session I attended, I was afraid of breaking this wonderful spell.

Finally, I could understand my spirit more deeply, Taoist Tai Chi felt like the circle I was living in was finally complete."

Lipstick Day

I was just 36 years old when I suffered my first 3 heart attacks. In the days that followed, I had to absorb so much information, that went from bad to the very worse that you can imagine.

"We don't think you've had a heart attack, you're too young"

"Well yes it was a heart attack but you won't have any more"

"Ok, so you've had 2 more heart attacks and you've now got heart failure"

"Umm....We think you should prepare your family, do you want to see your kids?"

"The world has blown up and your head is about to drop off....." Well, they didn't say that, but it wouldn't have surprised me.

In a nutshell my life as I knew it was over, or so I believed. I lay in a bed in intensive care, hooked up to monitors that constantly sent alarm bells ringing, literally. I was given no positive prognosis for survival at all.

I had 3 babies at home and no way of being well enough to get back to them.

Lipstick Day

However, when I was on day 10 of being in the hospital, a bright red lipstick became the epitome of my survival.

On this magical tenth day of my survival, a non-essential, superficial item shone out to me like a beacon from heaven.

My lovely mum brought me a red lipstick into the hospital and stood it up on my bedside table.

I swear it was winking at me! Whispering to me..."use me...I'm pretty....pick me up..."

At this stage, I wasn't allowed to pee, shower, or move, I wasn't allowed to do anything on my own. Because my heart was so badly damaged, one false move and it could give up the ghost completely.

But luckily, my mum knew me well.

She recognised that if I was going to survive this terrible trauma, then it would be down to my attitude, my determination and my stubbornness. She knew that I had to start fighting to get me back.

It worked.

Instead of lying in my hospital bed, accepting that my life was over, I suddenly demanded that I had my hair washed. I don't know where the urge came from, but believe me, it was strong. There were some big arguments about it, of course, my hair wasn't a priority for the medical staff, they just wanted me not to die. I didn't want to die either, but it was also really, really important to me that I had nice hair!

So, with medics and machinery on standby, my head was lowered off the end of the bed and my hair was washed.

It felt AMAZING!

I felt AMAZING!

I had taken control of my life in that moment, I had managed to put the Sally back in the Bee and achieve something so insignificant to many, yet so significant to me and my confidence.

I slept for a solid 16 hours after the effort, but it had been worth it, to feel that glimmer of hope for a future life. I had just proved to myself that if I could take control of this small 'insignificant' thing, having my hair washed so that I simply felt pretty, I could take control of the bigger things...like staying alive!

The doctors couldn't tell me I was going to be OK, but I had clean hair, and that meant I was back in the driving seat!

The next day, was lipstick day.

I woke up, and had my bed bath, given to me by a handsome male nurse – I smiled at him, lots. And then I asked for a mirror and put on the red lipstick that my mum had brought in the day before.

I was pale, lethargic, had dark eyes, and oxygen was being pumped up my nose...but I had clean, shiny hair and was wearing red lipstick. It was wonderfully liberating and life-changing.

How can something as superficial and non-essential as lipstick be so liberating? Surely, you might say, I had bigger things to think about? I was probably going to die. I had 3 young children and a husband who were going to have to manage without me...But this is what I learned, very quickly:

You can't change what happens to you, you can only change how you react to it.

Sometimes you have to accept a situation and not try to battle it. Give it respect, and then politely turn your back and change direction. Not every situation you end up in has to carry such significance.

We are all different, and whatever makes you smile in a single moment, is worth its weight in gold. A single happy moment will grow – but you have to feed it.

Even if you don't feel it, YOU are in control of YOU! You just need to find a way to remind yourself of who you are, and what you can achieve.

My red lipstick saved me, or at least it represented the beginning of my journey to save myself. It reminded me of the power I have over my fate and future. Of course, I understand that I cannot predict how long I am going to survive, but I can predict that I am going to continue loving my life, my family, and my friends and loving the pretty things that make me feel feminine and empowered in a single moment.

Today, my red lipstick still proves to me that no matter what I am facing, if I can still care enough about how I look, how I feel and how I present myself to the world, then it's not time to give up.

My red lipstick still gives me the strength to survive.

So the next time someone asks you whether things like make-up, clothes and all things pretty matter, and should you care about them? I hope you know the answer.

Listen To Your Heart

Words from Lyndsey Whiteside

"I nearly lost my life when my gorgeous baby boy was born 5 years ago. I was diagnosed with severe heart failure and told I wouldn't survive a year.

5 years later, I'm still here!

I take care to practise gratitude for my life and each new day. I make joy a priority. I shun stress and toxic relationships and I listen to my heart. I ask her what she wants - and take action when she wants to beat a little faster or a little slower.

I hold on to hope through fear and I have an indomitable love for life.

Be grateful that you are here and listen to your heart!"

The Big Picture

Faith And Spirituality

Am I religious?

Well, I understand the basic philosophies relating to different named religions but I don't live my life ruled by any one of them. I suppose I take some learning from each.

I struggle with the hierarchy in many religions because it seems that it is often based on rules of power and that goes against the grain for me. I believe that we are all equal in our views and thoughts and no one should be judged on their beliefs as right or wrong against another.

Having said that, I do feel that I have a faith and that I believe in a God. I believe that my God is the spirit that lives inside me.

My spirituality is the part of me that desires more. My spiritual side doesn't focus on the mundane, it helps me look at the big picture, and it helps me empathise with a deeper understanding of others. It allows me to feel an incredible sense of joy, aliveness and belonging to the planet. So, if I had to accept a name for my faith, I would call myself a Humanist. I care about people, animals and the planet.

When I tap into my spirituality, I feel connected and more able to delve into my thoughts and feelings. I feel light-hearted, which gives me the energy and space to show extra kindness to myself and those around me.

If ever I feel overwhelmed, I ask my God, my spirit, to guide me and give me strength and it has never let me down.

This is such a personal thing, that I don't want to fill your mind with my beliefs so much, but I do hope that you can look inside to find your faith and spirituality as this will connect you to something greater than yourself.

Finding your inner faith can help bring you joy and ease and will help you acknowledge that there is perhaps a bigger force at work in your life. Then you can stop trying to control everything and let your life unfold in ways that you might not dream are possible.

Hope And A Friend Called Clare

Words by Abbi Rendell

"I had hit rock bottom in a pretty dramatic way, but by finding the right kind of help, a friend named Clare who brought to me some hope, I'm back!

My story revolves around the birth of my amazing daughter, Daisy. She has always been perfect, but I didn't react well emotionally after having her. I knew this wasn't just post-natal depression. My mind was playing horrible tricks on me, voices told me how bad a mother I was and I was out of control. I couldn't trust myself.

Then, after many, many desperate hours of searching, I found Clare and with her came hope. I had by this point been diagnosed with post-natal psychosis and had been offered some medication that scared me just as much as the psychosis itself.

Clare had experience and I trusted her instantly because she could describe exactly how I felt. After all, she had felt it too. She promised me that I would get better, she taught me what to eat, how and when to move and ultimately she saved my life by offering me hope."

Hope is often the missing piece of your puzzle. But in order to find hope, you need to know what it is you are hoping for!

You are probably stronger than you realise, but being strong is really difficult when you don't know what you are dealing with and what you're up against.

Abbi began her journey to feeling better as soon as she was given her diagnosis of post-natal psychosis. She had to understand what the problem was before she could attract the right kind of help. She then met Clare who helped her realise she wasn't alone.

If you have something happening to you that doesn't feel right, if you instinctively know something is wrong, don't stop searching for the answer until you've found it!

Once you know exactly what you are dealing with, you can find your Clare to give you hope.

Books You Must Read

Opening a new book is like opening the door to your new mind; the mind you have yet to access. Who knows what you'll discover as you turn the next page? I sometimes read books with sad tears falling down my cheeks, sometimes I laugh so hard it hurts. You will already know what sort of book entices you, as literary choice is subjective, and you will have your favourites.

However, I urge you to occasionally step out of your comfort zone when choosing books. Get recommendations from people that have interesting stuff to say, it's likely they'll have some good ideas for you.

I remember one day, my mum telling me with great enthusiasm, that she was "going to read the classics". It had clearly been a determined decision for her.

At the time I must have been in my late teens and I can remember thinking, why? Why would anyone want to read something written so long ago, that it probably isn't at all relevant anymore? It made no sense to me at the time.

Well, I have just spent a year reading the classics and I LOVED every single precious, old-fashioned word.

So, I ask myself again, why?

I think what happened to me was that I reached a point in my life where I had no more room in my head or heart for the superficial or the meaningless.

I have taken in so much over the years, from books, shows, movies, and people, and I have come to realise that I have no appetite for it a moment longer.

Everything has its place in the world. I used to enjoy wiling away the hours watching endless soap operas, and trashy TV shows. I read hundreds of chic-lit novels, and I'm not saying these books were all meaningless, but I feel I got to the stage where I wanted to spend my time reading books that could teach me something new, challenge my mind, take me back in time and help me understand how we got to where we are today.

I think when you reach that saturation point of 'no more crap' (by the way, this happens in all aspects of your life, not just books) when you reach that point, it's wonderful; because you are then ready to read all the fantastic, educating, time travelling, historical, mind-blowing books.

When your time comes, when your shift in choice happens, you'll get it!

To Kill a Mockingbird

Harper Lee

While To Kill a Mockingbird is a favourite book of pretty much everyone who has read it, it's important to remember that it continues to be challenging to many readers. The protagonist is a young girl named Scout and except for her father, all the main characters in the book are controlled by the power structure of their town where wealthy white men control the lives of everyone else. Even the members of that group, who want to use their status for something honourable, like Scout's father Atticus, cannot win against the flattening wave of that power. A really thought-provoking read.

Lady Chatterley's Lover

D.H. Lawrence

This book was written (and banned!) in 1928. Before women had any say in pretty much anything, before they were allowed to vote and before any kind of global sexual revolution. Yet, amazingly, it was written, with a deep understanding of womanhood, by a man! The book is still banished from publication in India, probably because it unnerves the classic opinions of class and sex.

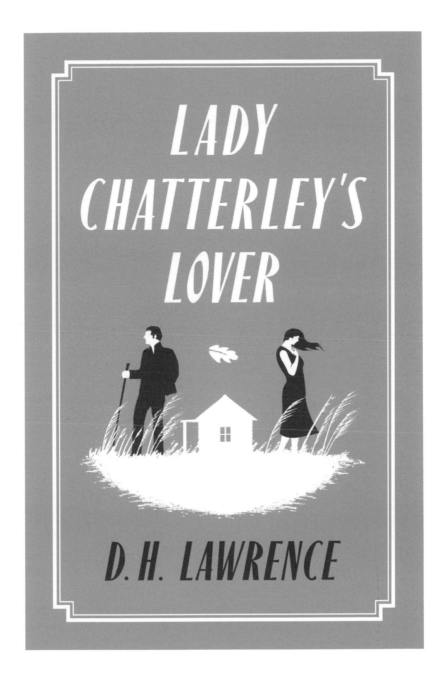

Little Women

Louisa May Alcott

Little Women is a beloved 19th-century classic that is still read today and is, I would imagine, loved by all. The novel is about four sisters who grow up together, with family love, sibling rivalries, and searching for their own identity. It's about love and relationships, poverty, wealth, priorities in life, and most importantly to me, focuses on female independence. Back in that time, a young woman could not compete with her male companions but this novel breaks that stereotype, beautifully.

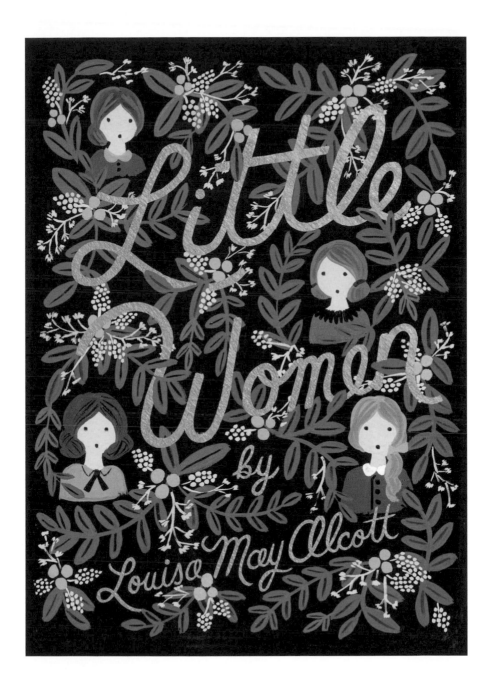

Places You Must Visit

Go everywhere your heart desires.

Always save some money for a rainy day, but don't spend it on that rainy day, spend it on a train or airline ticket to distant lands and cultures.

You must travel at every given opportunity. Discover your own routes and favourite vibes in cities and countryside alike. Travel with friends or go it alone. Don't spend all day in shops that you can find at home, go deeper, go to galleries, parks, historical places and museums.

Behave like a tourist on the first day and take the open-top bus tour. These are usually really great value for money, and allow you to get your bearings in a new city and see which places appeal to you most. Then on the second day, make like the locals, go off-piste, away from the tourist areas and discover the authentic people.

One of the most beautiful places I have visited is Mauritius. Besides the idyllic views and scenery, I was blown away by the clear, happy mixture of cultures. I sat drinking a lovely cold margarita, watching a beautiful Indian lady in a brightly coloured sari, greet her dear friend who was French. Her friend was sassy in shorts and a very cropped crop top. Two opposite ends of the cultural and fashion spectrum, who obviously shared a deep love and respect for one another.

I also loved Barbados with its beach shacks, turquoise water, and miles of white sandy beaches.

I visited Barbados with my job for ITV, filming some health and wellbeing segments. I think at this stage in my career, I had become a little blasé about travelling because I did it so often. However, I can remember feeling a sense of excitement brought on purely by the colours that danced in front of my eyes.

Everywhere I looked, every corner that I turned had yet another hue that took my breath away. Who knew there were so many different shades of turquoise, blue, green and yellow?

The buildings, huts and shacks, echoed the nature that sat around them, with flaking paint and weather-worn surfaces. The beautiful warm, natural Bajan light, made everything look a hundred times more beautiful compared to the dull shadow that is often cast over buildings in the UK.

Don't let other people's fear stop you. Work it out for yourself.

Rio De Janeiro, the capital of Brazil launches an attack on all your senses the very second you land! The heat, smells, visions, people, food, crowds, noises, emotions, and passions, all run super high in Rio.

I travelled to the most vibrant place on the planet for another filming trip with my TV show. Before we went, the crew and I were asked to adhere to the television company's strict safety requirements. These included, never leaving the hotel complex alone, never eating at restaurants that were not pre-checked and pre-booked and always staying with the crew and security guard assigned to us. We were taught how to get mugged, safely!?? and how to recognise a bandit!

Our security guard, Carlos, was an enormous chap, with huge bulging muscles, about 8ft tall, who, apparently, carried a loaded gun in his innocent-looking satchel! Just looking at him, scared the life out of me to begin with, but after my first gentlemanly rescue (no guns required, I simply tripped over my high heels and Carlos saved me!) he and I became firm friends.

After 4 days of following the rules, and sticking to Carlos like glue, I became a little restless and wanted to venture out alone. Carlos was busy polishing his gun (OK, that's not actually true, but you have to admit it sounds good!) So, I slipped out of the hotel lobby quietly with an equally naughty, rebellious producer called Katie. We were prepared to take our life in our hands, and experience the 'real' Rio.

And the 'real' Rio was wonderful.

Rio is a city with golden beaches and lush mountains. It is sophisticated yet raw. It is known for its samba-fuelled nightlife and spectacular football matches. Music is the lifeblood of Rio and you can hear it all over town. Visit the small juice bars that you'll see on every street corner and simply sit and watch this different world, move to its own rhythm.

You must visit Copacabana Beach which became a symbol of Rio during the 1940s when international starlets would jet in for the weekend. And then, of course, there's the famous, Ipanema Beach, where you can sit and watch the ocean while listening to 'The Girl From Ipanema'.

The Girl From Ipanema lyrics, so that you can sing along!

Tall and tan and young and lovely

The girl from Ipanema goes walking

And when she passes

Each one she passes goes "ah!"

When she walks she's like a samba that

Swings so cool and sways so gently

That when she passes,

Each one she passes goes "ah!"

Oh, but he watches her so sadly

How can he tell her he loves her?

Yes, he would give his heart gladly

But each day when she walks to the sea

She looks straight ahead not at him

Tall and tan and young and lovely

The girl from Ipanema goes walking

And when she passes he smiles

But she doesn't see

Oh, but he watches her so sadly

How can he tell her he loves her?

Yes, he would give his heart gladly

But each day when she walks to the sea

She looks straight ahead not at him

Tall and tan and young and lovely

The girl from Ipanema goes walking

And when she passes he smiles

But she doesn't see

She just doesn't see

No she doesn't see

She just doesn't see no, no

Although I've told you to travel where your heart takes you, you must also visit the classics!

Go to Paris.

Nonchalant. Hopeful. Stylish.

Springtime. The Yves Saint Laurent Museum. Galerias Lafayette. Sacre Coeur on a sunny day, the view is amazing. Notre Dame Site (being rebuilt after a devastating fire). Save up and eat at Le Train Bleu, the most beautiful restaurant at Gare De Lyon.

Go to New York.

Noisy. Exhilarating. Exhausting.

Brooklyn Bridge. Ground Zero. Central Park on a Sunday. Shopping in Soho. The Whispering Gallery in Grand Central Station. Eat at Katz's Delicatessen, Lower East Side.

Go to London.

Traditional. Theatrical. Cosmopolitan.

Liberty store. Pall Mall. Walk down Southbank on a sunny evening. Coffee and cake at Bar Italia in Soho. Columbia Road Flower Market. Brick Lane. Covent Garden Opera House.

It feels good to travel

and get lost

in the right direction

My Caveat on Travel: I am always super aware that you may not be able to afford to travel to some of these amazing places. I certainly couldn't have afforded them myself, they only happened because the trips were paid for through my job.

If you are not able to afford long-distance trips just now, you must still believe and dream and wish. Do your research, chose the places you would like to travel to, make plans and be determined that one day, you will find a way... and you, my darling, will.

3 Recipes In An Emergency

So, your quiet night in turns into an impromptu house party where no one wants to leave until 5am. You wake up at 11am, with a distant memory of dancing on the table, but no proof...you hope!

There are six very hungry people still in the house. No problem, you've got this covered.

Mexican Butterbean Hash

Serves 4

Ingredients

1 x 400g tin butter beans

2 tbsp extra virgin olive oil

1 medium onion, finely sliced

2 cloves garlic, peeled and crushed

4 lean rashers of bacon, all visible
fat cut off

2 tins of chopped tomatoes

4 preserved jalapenos, chopped

A slurp of Tabasco sauce, to taste

Freshly ground black pepper

4 fresh eggs

Method

Preheat the oven to 200°C. In a large non-stick frying pan, heat the olive oil over medium heat. Add the chopped onion and fry off for 4-5 minutes.

Next, add the bacon, garlic, chopped tomatoes and butter beans. Season with black pepper, chopped jalapenos and Tabasco sauce. Stir to combine and let simmer over low heat for 10-15 minutes.

Now, transfer the mixture to a shallow baking dish and pop it in the preheated oven for 20 minutes, until bubbling and all the flavours have fused together.

Take out of the oven and make 4 scooped holes in the mixture. Crack in the eggs and pop back in the oven for a final 6-7 minutes.

Serve piping hot with crusty, buttered bread.

Every girl needs to have a chocolate mousse recipe hiding up her sleeve. Chocolate is the food of love and is perfect for any special occasion. Practice until you have this recipe nailed.

Chocolate Mousse

(Delia Smith Recipe)
Serves 4

Ingredients

200g dark chocolate (75% cocoa
solids), broken into pieces

120ml warm water

3 large eggs, separated

40g golden caster sugar

Method

First of all place the broken-up chocolate and the warm water in a large heat-proof bowl, which should be sitting over a saucepan of barely simmering water, making sure the bowl doesn't touch the water.

Then, keeping the heat at its lowest, allow the chocolate to melt slowly – it should take about 6 minutes. Now remove it from the heat and give it a good stir until it's smooth and glossy, then let the chocolate cool for 2-3 minutes before stirring in the egg yolks. Then give it another good mix with a wooden spoon.

Next, in a clean bowl, whisk the egg whites to the soft-peak stage, then whisk in the sugar, about a third at a time, then whisk again until the whites are glossy.

Now, using a metal spoon, fold a tablespoon of the egg whites into the chocolate mixture to loosen it, then carefully fold in the rest. You need to have patience here – it needs gentle folding and cutting movements so that you retain all the precious air, which makes the mousse light.

Next, divide the mousse between the ramekins or glasses and chill for at least 2 hours, covered with clingfilm.

This dark, rich treat will be ready when you are.

When dinner guests drop by (maybe you have forgotten they are coming), this is the perfect dish to whip up in literally 10 minutes. Just send someone out to the nearby shop to pick up the fresh ingredients (The prawns you will already have in the freezer and these will defrost in no time) Meanwhile, you jump in the shower, super fast, and change into something comfortable but gorge! Then share a glass or two of wine, while you amaze your guests with your ease and skill! Delicious!

Seafood Linguine

Serves 4

Ingredients

280g linguine pasta

200g asparagus tips or sugar snap peas

2 tbsp olive oil

2 large garlic cloves, finely chopped

1 large red chilli, deseeded and finely chopped

24 raw king prawns, peeled

12 cherry tomatoes, halved

a handful of fresh basil leaves

mixed salad leaves and crusty white bread, to serve

For the lime dressing:

2 tbsp fromage frais

grated zest and juice of 2 limes

2 tsp golden caster sugar

Method

For the dressing, mix the fromage frais, caster sugar, lime zest and juice in a small bowl. Season with salt and pepper. Set aside.

Cook the pasta according to the packet instructions. Add the asparagus tips or sugar snap peas for the last minute or so of cooking time.

Meanwhile, heat the olive oil in a wok, toss in the garlic and chilli and cook over a medium heat for about 30 seconds without letting the garlic brown.

Next add the prawns and cook over a high heat, stirring frequently, for about 3 minutes until they turn pink.

Add the cherry tomatoes and cook for 3 minutes until they just start to soften.

Drain the linguine pasta, then toss into the prawn mixture. Add a handful of torn basil leaves and mix well.

Serve with mixed salad leaves drizzled with the lime dressing and enjoy.

My Last Words - Before My Next

Darling, don't ever expect life to be easy. It's not. But always expect it to be wonderful.

Wonderfully exciting.

Wonderfully sad.

Wonderfully fulfilling.

Wonderfully quiet.

Wonderfully happy.

Wonderfully tough,

Wonderfully alive.

Everything that happens to you, happens for a reason. Your past traumas will become your future strengths and your dreams, wishes and desires, sit just on the other side of fear.

You've got this, and I'm with you, all the way.

Until next time,

Sally Bee x

Huge thanks go to my wonderful family and team, my supporters and all contributors: Danielle Wittey, thank you for providing me with space to write, Tarik Halil, thank you for your amazing design input, I love this book almost as much as I love you! Thank you Paula Rowe, Jayne Clayton, Grace Haynes, Lyndsey Whiteside, Karen Williamson, Joanne Wood, Hayley Atkins, Suzy Elrick, Abbi Rendell, Margaret Whittaker and Hannah Smith for sharing your incredible stories. Thank you Tracy Lombard for your brilliant, ninja like editing. Thank you all! xxx

Picture Credits:

Pages 11, 19, 21, 31, 34, 35, 50, 56, 57, 74, 75, 86, 87, 177, 186, 187, 197, 212, 213, 218 - Various photographers, licensed through Shutterstock. Page 24 - © Twentieth Century Fox. Page 29 - © Vogue France. Page 96 - © John Clark. Page 102 - © Vanity Magazine. Page 105 - © Betty Paige. Page 145 - © Mike Horseman. All remaining images are either © Sally Bee or are in the public domain. If you have any queries about any of the images, please email publishing@mediadelicious.com

Chocolate Mousse Recipe Page page 222 © Delia Smith. The Girl From Ipanema lyrics pages 214-215 © Antonio Carlos Jobim.

SallyBee

 @sallybeehealthy

 @sallybeelicious

 @sallybeelicious

🌐 www.sally-bee.com